$ 3⁰⁰/(x)

S0-AQK-574

S0-AQK-574

$3.⁰⁰
3.—
④

INTERNATIONAL
Furniture
DESIGN
For the '90s

INTERNATIONAL
Furniture
DESIGN
For the '90s

The Library of Applied Design

PBC INTERNATIONAL

New York

Distributor to the book trade in the United States and Canada:

Rizzoli International Publications Inc.
300 Park Avenue South
New York, NY 10010

Distributor to the art trade in the United States:

PBC International, Inc.
One School Street
Glen Cove, NY 11542
1-800-527-2826
Fax 516-676-2738

Distributor to the art trade in Canada:

Letraset Canada Ltd.
170 Duffield Drive
Markham, Ontario, Canada L6G 1B5

Distributed throughout the rest of the world:

Hearst Books International
105 Madison Avenue
New York, NY 10016

Copyright © 1991 by
PBC INTERNATIONAL, Inc.
All rights reserved. No part of this book may be reproduced
in any form whatsoever without written permission of the
copyright owner, PBC INTERNATIONAL, INC.,
One School Street, Glen Cove, NY 11542.

International furniture design for the '90s /
edited PBC International.
     p.   cm.
    Includes index.
    ISBN 0-86636-136-7
    1. Furniture design--History--20th century.

NK2395.I57 1991
749.2'0400--dc20   90-27600
ISBN 0-86636-136-7   CIP

*CAVEAT—Information in this text is believed accurate, and
will pose no problem for the student or casual reader.
However, the author was often constrained by information
contained in signed release forms, information that could
have been in error or not included at all. Any
misinformation (or lack of information) is the result of failure
in these attestations. The author has done whatever is
possible to insure accuracy.*

For information about our audio products, write us at:
Newbridge Book Clubs, 3000 Cindel Drive, Delran, NJ 08370

Interior Book Design
Ronald Gabriel

Color separation, printing and binding by
Toppan Printing Co. (H.K.) Ltd. Hong Kong

Typography by
TypeLink, Inc.

10 9 8 7 6 5 4 3 2 1

The following quote was provided by Rick
Kaufmann/ART et INDUSTRIE.

"…if our houses, furniture and utensils are not
works of art, they are either wretched make-
shifts, or, what is worse, degrading shams of
better things. Furthermore, if any of these
things make claim to be considered works of
art, they must show obvious traces of the hand
of man guided directly by his brain, without
more inter-position of machines than is abso-
lutely necessary to the nature of the work
done. Again, whatsoever art there is in any of
these articles of daily use must be evolved in
a natural and unforced manner from the material that is dealt with, so that the result will
be such as could not be got from any other
material: if we break this law we make a trivi-
ality, a toy, not a work of art. Lastly, love of .
nature in all its forms must be the ruling spirit
of such works of art as we are considering;
the brain that guides the hand must be
healthy and hopeful, must be keenly alive to
the surroundings of our own days, and must
be only so much affected by the art of past
times as it is natural for one who practices an
art which is alive, growing and looking to-
wards the future."
"Hopes and Fears of Art"
William Morris
1882 — London

Contents

Introduction

The future of product design and the fate of the technology, art and craft that lend it coherent form, parallels the development and degeneration of culture. At the most essential level, at its intellectual core, the culture of this century that is about to end has been molded by the idea of modernism; the application of reason, law and science in the service of the progressive improvement of the conditions of human life. From the nineteenth century this notion of modernism has been under critical attack by both the right and the left.

With the end of the Cold War, however, and the collapse of the notion of historic and economic inevitability, the ideological orthodoxies of the right and left have been relocated to academia leaving us in the grip of a world market, an international mercantilist structure riddled by a lack of certainty or faith thanks to this century's legacy of war, genocide, barbarity, pollution and waste.

Is this the result of modernism? Are these brutal voices inherent in industrial mass production, in the idea of human 'progress' and in the means of its realization—the assembly line? Postmodernism says yes. It claims that modernism is ecologically unsound, authoritarian, a deluded fanaticism that strips down all forms, ideas and differences until they attain transparency, weightlessness, a repressive sameness, and then it pushes us into a nihilistic endgame, the choice of either/or: total meaning or no meaning at all.

The postmodernism of the 70's and 80's sought to replenish the meaning drained from cultural objects by modernism's reductive tendency by the appropriation of past styles. In the arena of forms and objects, buildings and products, postmodernism served as a creative tonic, allowing the emergence of a profusion of recombinant design strategies. None of them did anything to alter the hardware of our contemporary world, the manufacturing technique and social structure put in place by modernism.

It has been said that the essence of civilization, Oriental, Western, living and dead is restraint. In the last century we have learned the necessity of living within limits politically, economically and emotionally.

Postmodernism, the dominant intellectual trend of the past two decades, postulates constant critical opposition to all absolutes, in the hope of attaining a truly secular society, a culture of 'liberation' where authority is subverted, where no group or group of ideas can ever again attain mental dominance in the way rationalism and modernism became cannonized.

Product design lies at the intersection of industrialism, art, craft and the science of ergonomics. This makes it an ideal testing ground for a synthesis of an environmentally alert modernism and a license giving postmodernism. The many genies modernism has unleashed upon our overcrowded world may be tamed by self-imposed restraint. This is not to say that our freedom to imagine and invent and our expectations from life need to be austere or constricted. On the contrary. We need to fully exercise our imagination and creativity, to construct challenging and fanciful prototypes and to fully think through the consequences of what we are doing, making, building, before we act in a world where each of us is nothing more than a temporary guest.

Lois Lambert
Director, The Gallery of Functional Art
Santa Monica, California

THE GALLERY of FUNCTIONAL ART

"The artist thinks by way of relations"
—Theo Van Doesburg, 1917

There is no where more appropriate to experience first hand the dialectical relationship between art and object than at the Gallery of Functional Art. Located at 2429 Main St., at Edgemar, designed by Frank Gehry, in the heart of Santa Monica, the Gallery has become the focal point for outstanding functional art in the United States.

Inaugurated in August 1988, the Gallery of Functional Art has consistently held outstanding exhibitions of art furniture and other functional objects. The Director, Lois Lambert, assembles excellent collections by fine artists and architects for each show, and the result has been exhibitions which are both unique and innovative.

The artists themselves come from around the world, each bringing his own sense of style and design. The artists work with a wide range of materials; from wood and glass to steel, stone, precious metals and found objects. They create new conceptions of chairs, tables, mirrors, screens, lights and other practical items. The art works are available as either one-of-a-kind or limited edition pieces. In addition, one may peruse through the Gallery's extensive slide catalogue which is available by appointment.

During a recent interview with a design journalist, I expressed the view that, in creating an object, one should not pay attention to the market. Trained, educated and experienced, you listen only to your voice and create the object for itself. With prescience, the market will come to it. The journalist responded that this was asking the mountain to come to Mohammed, a purely romantic view in a society where astute designers are informed by, and create for, the market. This illustrates the current upside-down thinking in which we fail to perceive that the idea or the object is the mountain to which the market must come.

Our preoccupation with the market had its beginning well over a century ago, in the then seemingly romantic philosophy of William Morris who mated artisan and machine so as to make rarified objects available to a greater number of people. From a single artisan creating for 100, to one market-conscious designer creating for 100,000, we have come full cycle from a narrowcast to a broadcast society. Now that cycle has started to reverse itself.

The need to re-focus on a narrowcast approach became apparent with Europe's emerging presence as design leader in the 1960's. By then, American design had become subservient to mass-marketing and manufacturing concerns. The resulting incapacity for prototype development and short-run production fostered a demise in creativity and craft skills. The overt attention paid to the market diluted the conceptual and physical quality of our objects which, though more available, became increasingly disposable and ultimately less desirable.

Europe, while mistakenly restructuring toward the U.S. model, had a residual, though rapidly diminishing, base of small ateliers capable of creating prototypes and putting them into limited production for its still de-centralized market. The risk-taking and turnaround benefits of these seemingly outmoded cottage industries were Europe's creative and qualitative advantage.

Meanwhile, back in the States, saturated with shoddy and uninspired product, the '70s began to react. Lacking a network of small ateliers and faced with industry's indifference, creativity required an alternate approach. With the European prototype and its own vital arts scene as a model, creative American designers got back to their roots as artists, creating furniture as art. Concurrently the search for more honest forms of expression in the art world, prompted a number of American artists to return to their roots in the applied arts, creating art as furniture. Europeans followed suit and transformed their creative format from make-shift prototype to fully resolved art work.

For the first time since the Bauhaus, the right and left brain were re-connected, as artists and designers approached the same goal from opposite directions. The ends of design (specific and interactive) justified the means of the artist (intuitive and abstract). Together, the focus of design, energy of art and warmth of craft had combined to re-kindle and, in fact, re-invent the decorative arts. The past was perceived not as a grab bag of historical applique, but as the philosophical wellspring in the way of making things.

Historically, of necessity or desire, artists have always made furniture. By the 1980's artists' furniture had become a movement. The importance of individual vision was clearly expressed in the stylistic diversity of works connected, not by ideology or 'ism, but by simple originality and integrity. Minimalist or decorative, the unity of these objects is in their pluralism. Function is the framework, but the idea is varied beyond the formalist concerns of an avant-garde. It is art that is not in the image of art; it is an art that is something, not about something.

Hopefully in this last decade of the 20th century these unique art works and the deeper meaning they infer will balance the necessity of industry, while expanding the quality and diversity of its potential cornucopia. These objects honor the past in their relevant present and are windows to the future, stones whose waves will later reach the shore.

The decorative or applied arts are intrinsically real and potentially non-obsolescent things that, unlike fashion and technology, last. There is a definite need for permanence in an increasingly impermanent society, for works worthy of handing down through the generations. The idea is a new art, both of our times and timeless; meaningful objects of conceptual integrity that are meticulously crafted by one hand and passed to another. This care with which we create our objects for the 21st century can ensure that the future also has a future.

Rick Kaufmann
Director, Art et Industrie
New York, New York

ART et INDUSTRIE

Rick Kaufmann founded Art et Industrie in New York City's Soho district in 1977. The first gallery of furniture by artists, it helped define the new decorative art. It has consistently foreshadowed the future, as its exhibitions introduced the artists, materials and movements that influenced a generation. Emilio Ambasz has described the members of Art et Industrie as "exquisite birds in a zoo full of hippopotami."

From 1970–1977 Rick Kaufmann was co-director of Kaufmann/Rust Decorative Arts Int'l. From 1968–1970 he directed Mr. Spitz Antiques in Ann Arbor, Michigan.

The artists represented by Art et Industrie are:

Ron Arad, Norman Campbell, Jim Cole, Michele Oka Doner, James Evanson, Dan Friedman, James Hong, Laura Johnson, Gloria Kisch, Alex Locadia, Paul Ludick, Terence Main, Howard Meister, Forrest Myers, Robert Ryan, Peter Shire, Richard Snyder, Carmen Spera, Jonathan Teasdale, and Eleonora Triguboff.

CHAPTER

1
Chairs
Sofas
Stools
Benches

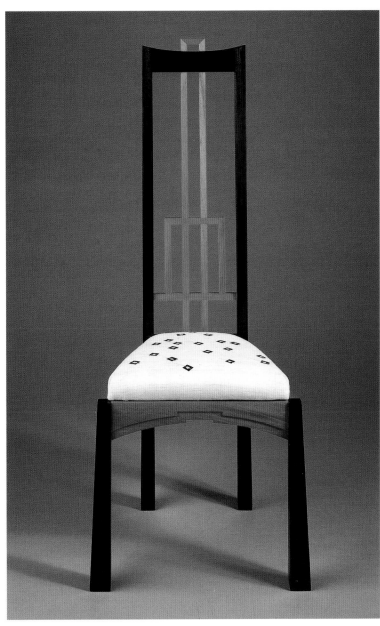

PRODUCT
ORIENTAL CHAIR
DESIGNER
BETH YOE
FIRM
CUTTING EDGE
MANUFACTURER
CUTTING EDGE
PHOTO
TOM FREEDMAN

PRODUCT
"JANUARY" SOFA
DESIGNER
SHIGERU UCHIDA
FIRM
STUDIO 80
MANUFACTURER
CHAIRS
DESCRIPTION
3-PERSON SOFA
PHOTO
NACÁSA & PARTNERS INC.

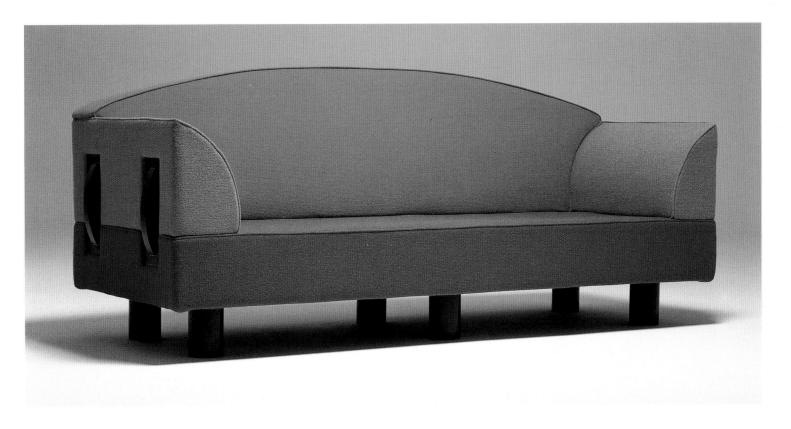

PRODUCT
HOUSE CHAIR
DESIGNER
FREDERIC SCHWARTZ
FIRM
ANDERSON SCHWARTZ
ARCHITECTS
PHOTO
STEVE MOORE

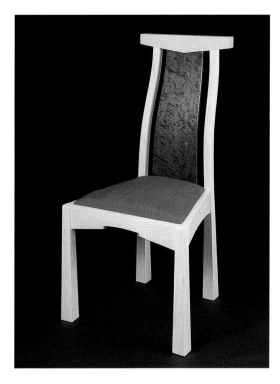

PRODUCT
REGIS CHAIR
DESIGNER
BETH YOE

PRODUCT
MUSICAL CHAIRS
DESIGNER
LLOYD SCHWAN
FIRM
GODLEY-SCHWAN
MANUFACTURER
GODLEY-SCHWAN
PHOTO
JOHN DeLUCA

PRODUCT
WRAP CHAIR
DESIGNER
JAMES HONG
DESCRIPTION
LACQUERED STEEL
CLIENT
*AVAILABLE THROUGH ART
ET INDUSTRIE*
PHOTO
JOSEPH COSCIA, JR.

PRODUCT
3 CHAIRS
DESIGNER
JOEL SOKOLOV
PHOTO
JOEL SOKOLOV

PRODUCT
"JULY" CHAIR
DESIGNER
SHIGERU UCHIDA
FIRM
STUDIO 80
MANUFACTURER
CHAIRS
PHOTO
NACÁSA & PARTNERS INC.

PRODUCT
*CHINESE MACINTOSH
CHAIR*
DESIGNER
BETH YOE
FIRM
CUTTING EDGE
MANUFACTURER
CUTTING EDGE
PHOTO
DAVID L. BROWN

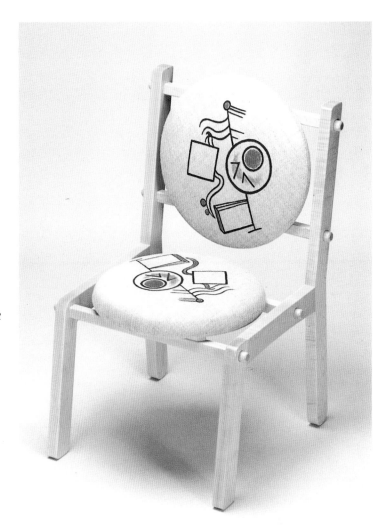

PRODUCT
DELBANCO CHAIR
DESIGNER
KURT DELBANCO

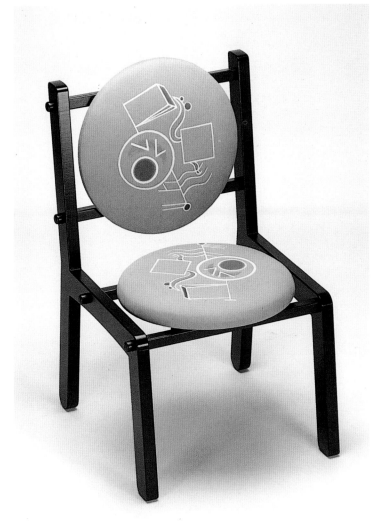

PRODUCT
"MARCH" CHAIR
DESIGNER
SHIGERU UCHIDA
FIRM
STUDIO 80
MANUFACTURER
CHAIRS
PHOTO
NACÁSA & PARTNERS INC.

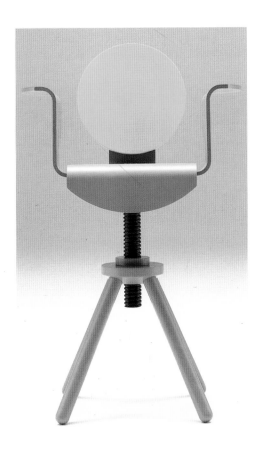

PRODUCT
"AUGUST" CHAIR
DESIGNER
SHIGERU UCHIDA
FIRM
STUDIO 80
MANUFACTURER
CHAIRS
PHOTO
NACÁSA & PARTNERS INC.

PRODUCT
HOLE CHAIR
DESIGNER
LAURA JOHNSON
DESCRIPTION
*CAST BRONZE,
LACQUERED WOOD
AND STEEL*
CLIENT
*AVAILABLE THROUGH ART
ET INDUSTRIE*
PHOTO
JOSEPH COSCIA, JR.

PRODUCT
ETHEL
DESIGNER
PAUL LUDICK
DESCRIPTION
*RAW SILK AND WOOD
CHAIR*
CLIENT
*AVAILABLE THROUGH ART
ET INDUSTRIE*
PHOTO
JOSEPH COSCIA, JR.

PRODUCT
"OCTOBER" CHAIR
DESIGNER
SHIGERU UCHIDA
FIRM
STUDIO 80
MANUFACTURER
CHAIRS
PHOTO
NACÁSA & PARTNERS INC.

PRODUCT
STONE THRONE
DESIGNER
NORMAN CAMPBELL
DESCRIPTION
*WOOD, FORGED STEEL
AND STONE CHAIR*
CLIENT
*AVAILABLE THROUGH ART
ET INDUSTRIE*
PHOTO
JOSEPH COSCIA, JR.

PRODUCT
LEAVES OFF/LEGS UP
DESIGNER
PAUL LUDICK
DESCRIPTION
*MAPLE AND CHERRY
CHAIR*
CLIENT
*AVAILABLE THROUGH ART
ET INDUSTRIE*
PHOTO
JOSEPH COSCIA, JR.

PRODUCT
DEMETER
DESIGNER
HOWARD MEISTER
DESCRIPTION
*HAND WROUGHT
ALUMINUM CHAIR*
CLIENT
*AVAILABLE THROUGH ART
ET INDUSTRIE*
PHOTO
JOSEPH COSCIA, JR.

PRODUCT
JO-JO CHAIR
DESIGNER
JOSEPH FOSTER
DESCRIPTION
*PAINTED STEEL, MOLDED
PLYWOOD SEAT. SIGNED
AND NUMBERED LIMITED
EDITION OF 100*
CLIENT
*AVAILABLE THROUGH
FULLSCALE*
PHOTO
PEDRO RIBA

23

PRODUCT
LADDER CHAIR
DESIGNER
INDIA MAHDAVI
DESCRIPTION
BLACK PAINTED STEEL
UPHOLSTERED IN LEATHER.
ADJUSTABLE SEAT HEIGHT
CLIENT
AVAILABLE THROUGH
FULLSCALE

PRODUCT
AMBASSADOR CHAIR
DESIGNER
MICHAEL WOLK
FIRM
MICHAEL WOLK DESIGN ASSOCIATES
MANUFACTURER
LOARDS UPHOLSTERY, INC.
DESCRIPTION
FULLY-UPHOLSTERED, EXPOSED CHERRY LEGS
PHOTO
NANCY WATSON
AWARD
FLORIDA STYLE FURNITURE DESIGN COMPETITION, 1990—1ST PLACE— UPHOLSTERY CATEGORY

PRODUCT
CARDINAL RICHELIEU
DESIGNER
FORREST MYERS
DESCRIPTION
*ANODIZED ALUMINUM
ARM CHAIR*
CLIENT
*AVAILABLE THROUGH ART
ET INDUSTRIE*
PHOTO
JOSEPH COSCIA, JR.

PRODUCT
BLUE STONE
DESIGNER
FORREST MYERS
DESCRIPTION
*ANODIZED ALUMINUM
CHAIR*
CLIENT
*AVAILABLE THROUGH ART
ET INDUSTRIE*
PHOTO
JOSEPH COSCIA, JR.

PRODUCT
*ARMCHAIR (BEAST
COLLECTION)*
DESIGNER
DAVID SHAW NICHOLLS
FIRM
*DAVID SHAW NICHOLLS
CORP.*
DISTRIBUTOR
MODERN AGE

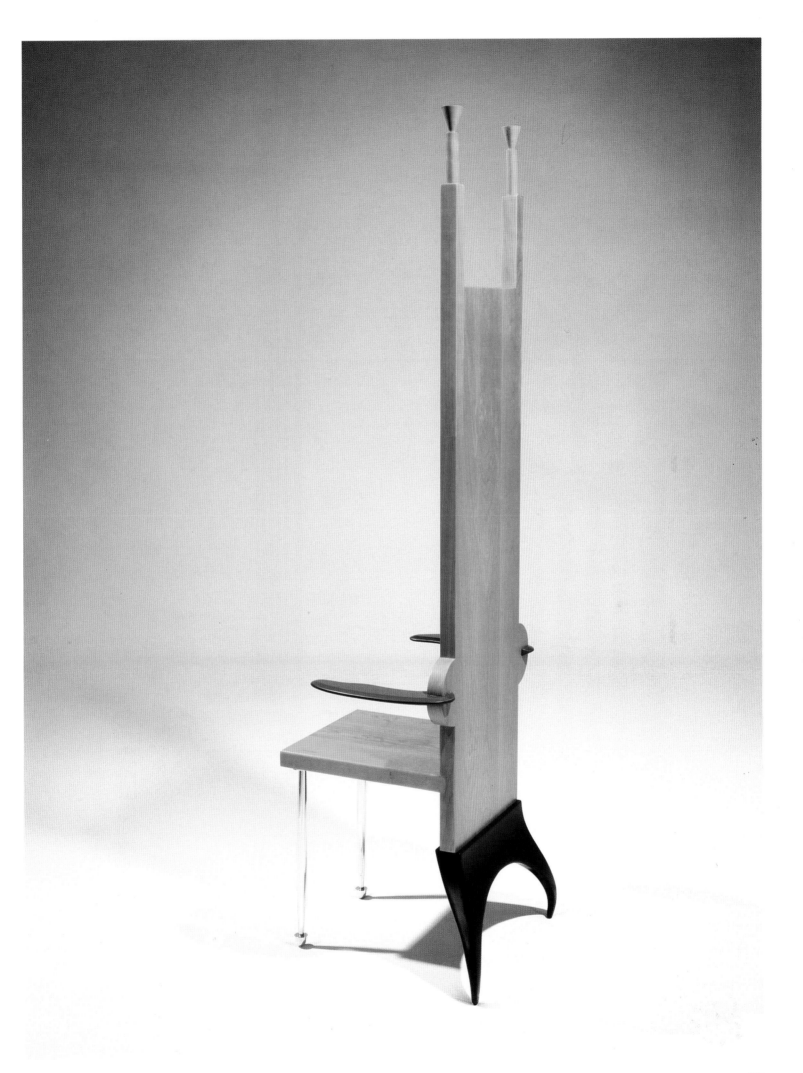

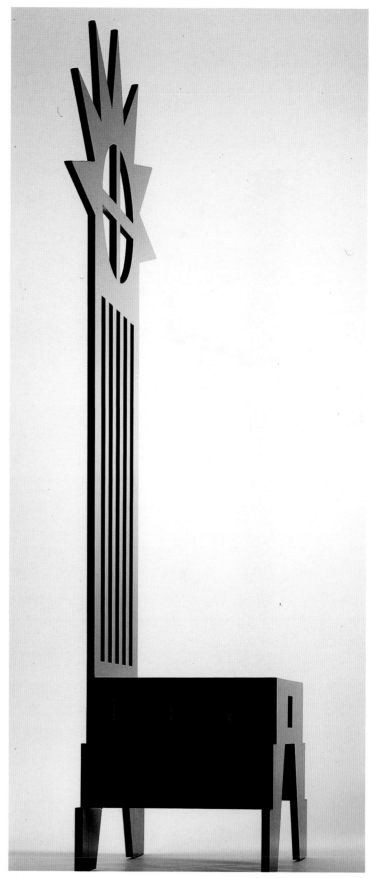

PRODUCT
SKYSCRAPER CHAIR
DESIGNER
FREDERIC SCHWARTZ
FIRM
ANDERSON/SCHWARTZ
ARCHITECTS
MANUFACTURER
TANSUNYA
PHOTO
STEVE MOORE

PRODUCT
TUCKER
DESIGNER
MICHAEL WOLK
FIRM
*MICHAEL WOLK DESIGN
ASSOCIATES*
MANUFACTURER
DESIGN AMERICA, INC.
DESCRIPTION
*UPHOLSTERED CHAIR IN
LEATHER, EXPOSED MAPLE
LEGS*
PHOTO
GREG FAWBUSH

PRODUCT
FORMAL CHAIR
DESIGNER
PAUL BRADLEY
FIRM
MATRIX PRODUCT DESIGN
DESCRIPTION
MAHOGANY FURNITURE
CLIENT
OBJECT DESIGN
PHOTO
RICK ENGLISH

PRODUCT
FAT FACE CHAIR
DESIGNER
GUIDO RODRIGUEZ
DESCRIPTION
*PAINTED STEEL FRAME
UPHOLSTERED WITH
LEATHER*
CLIENT
*AVAILABLE THROUGH
FULLSCALE*
PHOTO
F. STOPP

PRODUCT
LOVE SEAT
DESIGNER
DAVID PALESCHUCK
DESCRIPTION
*STAINLESS STEEL FRAME
WITH SILK UPHOLSTERY*
CLIENT
*AVAILABLE THROUGH
FULLSCALE*
PHOTO
PEDRO RIBA

PRODUCT
CHOW CHAIR
DESIGNER
ALLEN MIESNER
FIRM
MIESNER DESIGN

PRODUCT
HIROO CHAIR
DESIGNER
TOM FREEDMAN

PRODUCT
BLONGO CHAIR
DESIGNER
LEO J. BLACKMAN
MANUFACTURER
JOHN GONZALEZ
DESCRIPTION
WOOD CHAIR
PHOTO
RICHARD HACKETT
AWARD
*PURCHASED BY THE
BROOKLYN MUSEUM
FOR ITS PERMANENT
COLLECTION*

PRODUCT
CENTURY CITY
DESIGNER
MICHAEL WOLK
FIRM
*MICHAEL WOLK DESIGN
ASSOCIATES*
MANUFACTURER
DESIGN AMERICA, INC.
DESCRIPTION
*UPHOLSTERED CHAIR IN
LEATHER, EXPOSED MAPLE
ARMS*
PHOTO
GREG FAWBUSH

PRODUCT
ELROY CHAIR
DESIGNER
RHEA ALEXANDER
DESCRIPTION
*CAST ALUMINUM
WITH TEXTURED
ALUMINUM SEAT*
CLIENT
*AVAILABLE THROUGH
FULLSCALE*

PRODUCT
LOVE-SEAT WITH 5 LEGS
DESIGNER
JOEL SOKOLOV
DESCRIPTION
*PAINTED WOOD, SILK-
SCREENED FABRIC*
PHOTO
JOEL SOKOLOV

PRODUCT
THE MIAMI CHAIR
DESIGNER
MICHAEL WOLK
FIRM
*MICHAEL WOLK DESIGN
ASSOCIATES*
MANUFACTURER
LOARDS UPHOLSTERY, INC.
DESCRIPTION
*FULLY-UPHOLSTERED
CHAIR IN LEATHER*
PHOTO
BOB GELBERG
AWARD
*GRAND PRIZE WINNER OF
THE 1990 FLORIDA STYLE
FURNITURE DESIGN
COMPETITION*

PRODUCT
CONCCHELIA
DESIGNER
ELEONORA TRIGUBOFF
DESCRIPTION
PATINATED BRONZE CHAIR
CLIENT
*AVAILABLE THROUGH ART
ET INDUSTRIE*
PHOTO
BEVERLY PARKER

PRODUCT
ROADS
DESIGNER
ELEONORA TRIGUBOFF
DESCRIPTION
*ALUMINUM AND
AMARANTH CHAIR*
CLIENT
*AVAILABLE THROUGH ART
ET INDUSTRIE*
PHOTO
BEVERLY PARKER

37

PRODUCT
*"GAVINA" STOOL (VIEW
FROM RIGHT ANGLE)*
DESIGNER
JAIME TRESSERRA
FIRM
J. TRESSERRA DESIGN S.L.

PRODUCT
*RHODA SOFA AND
OSWALD CHAIR*
DESIGNER
ALEXIS DE LA FALAISE
CLIENT
*U.S. REPRESENTATIVE—
SARA VASS*

PRODUCT
"MS. MYSTERIOSO" CHAIR
DESIGNER
DAVID GALE
MANUFACTURER
DAVID GALE
DESCRIPTION
*STEEL TUBING, WELDED;
CLEAR-COATED*
CLIENT
*GALLERY OF FUNCTIONAL
ART*

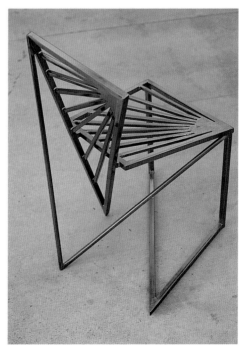

PRODUCT
OTTOMAN
DESIGNER
STEPHEN HARA
DESCRIPTION
*COPPER BASE WITH A
STEEL FRAME.
UPHOLSTERED IN
HORSEHAIR*
CLIENT
*AVAILABLE THROUGH
FULLSCALE*

PRODUCT
VEGA
DESIGNER
ALEX LOCADIA
DESCRIPTION
*METAL, ALUMINUM AND
LEATHER CHAIR*
CLIENT
*AVAILABLE THROUGH ART
ET INDUSTRIE*
PHOTO
JOSEPH COSCIA, JR.

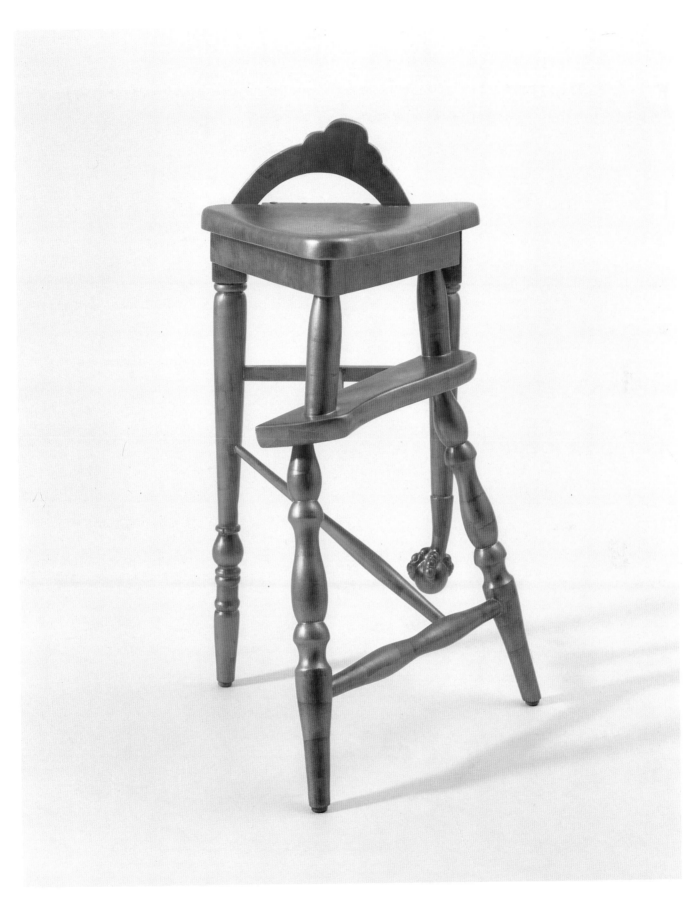

PRODUCT
STEWL
DESIGNER
DAVID PERRY
DESCRIPTION
WOOD AND COPPERLEAF
PHOTO
SUSAN EINSTEIN

PRODUCT
STOOL
DESIGNER
IRIS FINGERHUT
DESCRIPTION
*MAHOGANY, LACEWOOD,
WENGE*
PHOTO
NICOLE KATANO

PRODUCT
PHYSICS CHAIR
DESIGNER
MICHELE OKA DONER
DESCRIPTION
*RAW BRONZE AND BLACK
LEGS*
CLIENT
*AVAILABLE THROUGH ART
ET INDUSTRIE*
PHOTO
JOSEPH COSCIA, JR.

PRODUCT
ARGIANO CHAIR
DESIGNER
ALEXIS DE LA FALAISE
CLIENT
*U.S. REPRESENTATIVE—
SARA VASS*

43

PRODUCT
COMODA ARM CHAIR
DESIGNER
MAURIZIO PEREGALLI
FIRM
ZEUS COLLECTION—NOTO
MANUFACTURER
NOTO

DESCRIPTION
STEEL SQUARE TUBE STRUCTURE, EPOXY PAINTED BLACK. REVOLVING BACK AND SEAT BOTH IN BLACK SELF-SKINNING POLYURETHANE OR BENT BIRCH WOOD.
PHOTO
BITETTO-CHIMENTI

PRODUCT
EASY CHAIR
DESIGNER
WILL STONE
FIRM
LEWIS DOLIN, INC.
MANUFACTURER
WILL STONE
PHOTO
JASON JONES

PRODUCT
MUSICAL CHAIRS
DESIGNER
LLOYD SCHWAN
FIRM
GODLEY-SCHWAN
DESCRIPTION
SIDE CHAIRS
PHOTO
JOHN DeLUCA

45

PRODUCT
"JANUARY" SOFA
DESIGNER
SHIGERU UCHIDA
FIRM
STUDIO 80
MANUFACTURER
CHAIRS
PHOTO
NACÁSA & PARTNERS INC.

PRODUCT
"MODERN G" BARSTOOL
DESIGNER
DAVID MOCARSKI
FIRM
TACTION DESIGN
PHOTO
CHARLES IMSTEPF

PRODUCT
"SPANNER" CHAIR
DESIGNER
DAVID MOCARSKI
FIRM
TACTION DESIGN
DESCRIPTION
ARMCHAIR AND FOOTSTOOL
PHOTO
CHARLES IMSTEPF

PRODUCT
SCHOOL BUDDIES (BACK VIEW)
DESIGNER
TOM FREEDMAN
FIRM
CUTTING EDGE
MANUFACTURER
CUTTING EDGE
PHOTO
TOM FREEDMAN

47

PRODUCT
*911 FINESTRA ARMCHAIR
AND 910 OCULUS
ARMCHAIR*
DESIGNER
MICHAEL GRAVES
FIRM
*ATELIER INTERNATIONAL,
LTD.*
MANUFACTURER
*ATELIER INTERNATIONAL,
LTD.*
DESCRIPTION
*WOOD FRAME PULL-UP
CHAIR OFFERED IN
VARIOUS FINISHES AND
UPHOLSTERY*
PHOTO
*STUDIO PHOTOGRAPHERS
IN ITALY*

PRODUCT
PHYSICS BENCH
DESIGNER
MICHELE OKA DONER
DESCRIPTION
BRONZE BENCH
CLIENT
*AVAILABLE THROUGH ART
ET INDUSTRIE*
PHOTO
JOSEPH COSCIA, JR.

PRODUCT
COSMIC RAY CHAIR
DESIGNER
SHOZO TOYOHISA
FIRM
*EASTERN ACCENT
INTERNATIONAL INC.*
DESCRIPTION
*MADE OF IRON, LEATHER
AND STAINLESS WIRE*
DISTRIBUTOR
*EASTERN ACCENT
INTERNATIONAL INC.*

PRODUCT
"NOVEMBER" CHAIR
DESIGNER
SHIGERU UCHIDA
FIRM
STUDIO 80
MANUFACTURER
CHAIRS
PHOTO
NACÁSA & PARTNERS INC.

PRODUCT
"DECEMBER" CHAIR
DESIGNER
SHIGERU UCHIDA
FIRM
STUDIO 80
MANUFACTURER
CHAIRS
PHOTO
NACASA & PARTNERS INC.

PRODUCT
SUNDAY SETTEE
DESIGNER
GUIDO RODRIGUEZ
DESCRIPTION
*PLUM PATINATED STEEL
FRAME UPHOLSTERED
WITH LEATHER*
CLIENT
*AVAILABLE THROUGH
FULLSCALE*
PHOTO
BETH LUDWIG

PRODUCT
CORNER CHAIR
DESIGNER
DAVID PALESCHUCK
DESCRIPTION
TEXTURE PAINTED STEEL
WITH QUILTED
UPHOLSTERY. SIGNED AND
NUMBERED LIMITED
EDITION OF 100
CLIENT
AVAILABLE THROUGH
FULLSCALE
PHOTO
BETH LUDWIG

PRODUCT
CHAIR
DESIGNER
LESLIE GUBITOSI
DESCRIPTION
BLACK PAINTED STEEL
WITH A PURPLE HEART
WOOD SEAT
CLIENT
AVAILABLE THROUGH
FULLSCALE

PRODUCT
*OLA STACKING CHAIR
DESIGN (TWO BLACK, ONE
RED)*
DESIGNER
VLAD MÜLLER MA
FIRM
*MULLER ULLMANN
INDUSTRIAL DESIGN*
MANUFACTURER
*GLOBAL UPHOLSTERY CO.,
LTD.*
DESCRIPTION
*HIGH DENSITY STACKING,
GANGING CHAIR*
PHOTO
YURI DOJC

PRODUCT
211 DINING CHAIR
DESIGNER
GUIDO RODRIGUEZ
DESCRIPTION
*PLUM PATINATED STEEL
FRAME UPHOLSTERED
WITH LEATHER. SIGNED
AND NUMBERED LIMITED
EDITION OF 100*
CLIENT
*AVAILABLE THROUGH
FULLSCALE*
PHOTO
PEDRO RIBA

PRODUCT
*ARMCHAIR CIGARRA,
DEDOS TENIDOS
COLLECTION*
DESIGNER
ROBERTO LAZZERONI
FIRM
CECCOTTI COLLEZIONE
MANUFACTURER
CECCOTTI COLLEZIONE
DESCRIPTION
*SOLID CHERRY WOOD,
BLACK PAINTED*
CLIENT
CECCOTTI COLLEZIONE
PHOTO
MARIO CIAMPI
DISTRIBUTOR
FREDERIC WILLIAMS

PRODUCT
*CHAIR CHUMBERA, DEDOS
TENIDOS COLLECTION*
DESIGNER
ROBERTO LAZZERONI
FIRM
CECCOTTI COLLEZIONE
MANUFACTURER
CECCOTTI COLLEZIONE
DESCRIPTION
*SOLID CHERRY WOOD,
BLACK PAINTED*
CLIENT
CECCOTTI COLLEZIONE
PHOTO
MARIO CIAMPI
DISTRIBUTOR
FREDERIC WILLIAMS

PRODUCT
LOISAIDA CHAIR
DESIGNER
IRIS DeMAURO
FIRM
GEO INTERNATIONAL
CLIENT
GEO INTERNATIONAL
PHOTO
VICTOR SCHRAGER

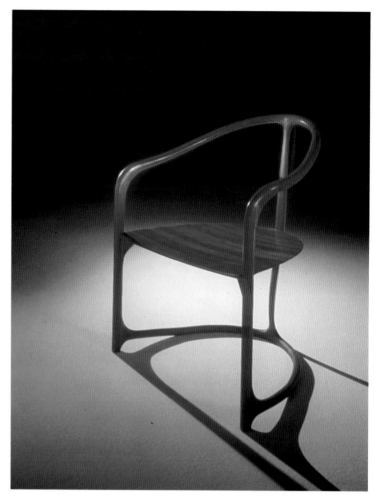

PRODUCT
DAMAS
DESIGNER
JEANNOT CERUTTI
FIRM
CECCOTTI COLLEZIONE
MANUFACTURER
CECCOTTI COLLEZIONE
DESCRIPTION
*ARMCHAIR OF SOLID
PADAUK WOOD WITH A
WAX FINISH*
CLIENT
CECCOTTI COLLEZIONE
PHOTO
MARIO CIAMPI
DISTRIBUTOR
FREDERIC WILLIAMS

PRODUCT
SARA CHAIR
DESIGNER
LEWIS DOLIN
FIRM
LEWIS DOLIN, INC.
MANUFACTURER
LEWIS DOLIN, INC.
DESCRIPTION
BLACK-STAINED
MAHOGANY FRAME
AND ANILIN-DYED
LEATHER SEAT. ARMS ARE
DESIGNED TO FIT UNDER A
DINING TABLE
PHOTO
JASON JONES

PRODUCT
CORNERWOOD CHAIR
DESIGNER
MICHAEL WOLK
FIRM
*MICHAEL WOLK DESIGN
ASSOCIATES*
MANUFACTURER
LOARDS UPHOLSTERY, INC.
DESCRIPTION
*FULLY-UPHOLSTERED
CHAIR WITH EXPOSED
CHERRY ARMS*
PHOTO
NANCY WATSON
AWARD
*MIAMI STYLE FURNITURE
DESIGN COMPETITION,
1988—3RD PLACE—
OVERALL*

PRODUCT
BAISITY SEATING SYSTEMS
DESIGNER
ANTONIO CITTERIO
MANUFACTURER
B & B ITALIA
PHOTO
ALDO BALLO

PRODUCT
BAISITY SEATING SYSTEMS
DESIGNER
ANTONIO CITTERIO
MANUFACTURER
B & B ITALIA
PHOTO
ALDO BALLO

PRODUCT
HOLLINGTON CHAIR
DESIGNER
GEOFF HOLLINGTON
FIRM
HOLLINGTON ASSOCIATES
MANUFACTURER
HERMAN MILLER INC.
U.S.A.
DESCRIPTION
LOUNGE CHAIR AND
OTTOMAN
CLIENT
HERMAN MILLER INC.
U.S.A.

PRODUCT
ST. JAMES™ CLUB CHAIR
FIRM
DONGHIA
DESCRIPTION
HIGH THRONE-LIKE BACK
AND ELONGATED ARMS
FOR HIGH STYLE AND
COMFORT
PHOTO
DONGHIA

PRODUCT
BAISITY SEATING SYSTEMS
DESIGNER
ANTONIO CITTERIO
MANUFACTURER
B & B ITALIA
PHOTO
ALDO BALLO

PRODUCT
BAISITY SEATING SYSTEMS
DESIGNER
ANTONIO CITTERIO
MANUFACTURER
B & B ITALIA
PHOTO
ALDO BALLO

PRODUCT
BREVET CHAIR
DESIGNER
MICHAEL WOLK
FIRM
*MICHAEL WOLK DESIGN
ASSOCIATES*
MANUFACTURER
LOARDS UPHOLSTERY, INC.
DESCRIPTION
*FULLY-UPHOLSTERED
CHAIR WITH EXPOSED OAK
ARMS*
PHOTO
GREG FAWBUSH

PRODUCT
BAISITY SEATING SYSTEMS
DESIGNER
ANTONIO CITTERIO
MANUFACTURER
B & B ITALIA
PHOTO
ALDO BALLO

PRODUCT
BAISITY SEATING SYSTEMS
DESIGNER
ANTONIO CITTERIO
MANUFACTURER
B & B ITALIA
PHOTO
ALDO BALLO

PRODUCT
SITY (SEATING SYSTEM)
DESIGNER
ANTONIO CITTERIO
MANUFACTURER
B & B ITALIA
PHOTO
G. PIERRE MAURER

PRODUCT
BAISITY SEATING SYSTEMS
DESIGNER
ANTONIO CITTERIO
MANUFACTURER
B & B ITALIA
PHOTO
ALDO BALLO

PRODUCT
SITY (SEATING SYSTEM)
DESIGNER
ANTONIO CITTERIO
MANUFACTURER
B & B ITALIA
PHOTO
G. PIERRE MAURER

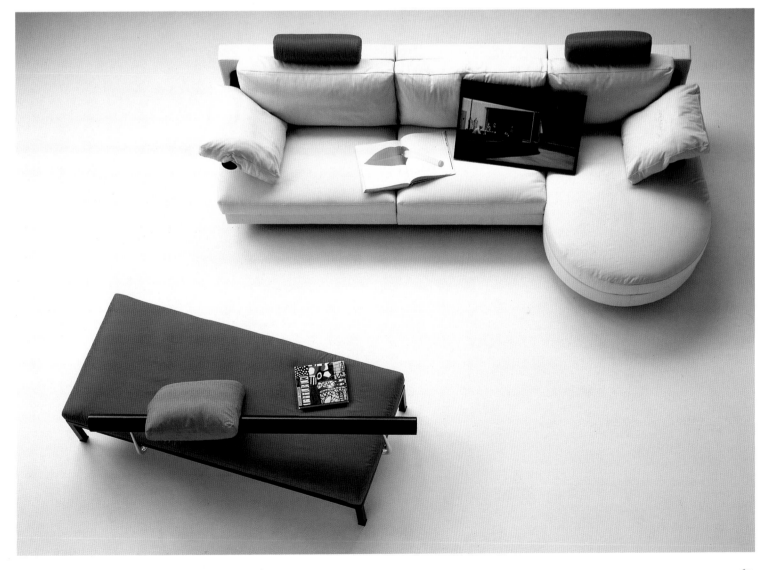

65

PRODUCT
BAISITY SEATING SYSTEMS
DESIGNER
ANTONIO CITTERIO
MANUFACTURER
B & B ITALIA
PHOTO
ALDO BALLO

PRODUCT
JUGENDSTIL COLLECTION
(SOFA, COFFEE TABLE...)
DESIGNER
BERND MÜNZEBROCK
MANUFACTURER
GEIGER INT'L
CLIENT
GEIGER INT'L

PRODUCT
SITY (SEATING SYSTEM)
DESIGNER
ANTONIO CITTERIO
MANUFACTURER
B & B ITALIA
PHOTO
G. PIERRE MAURER

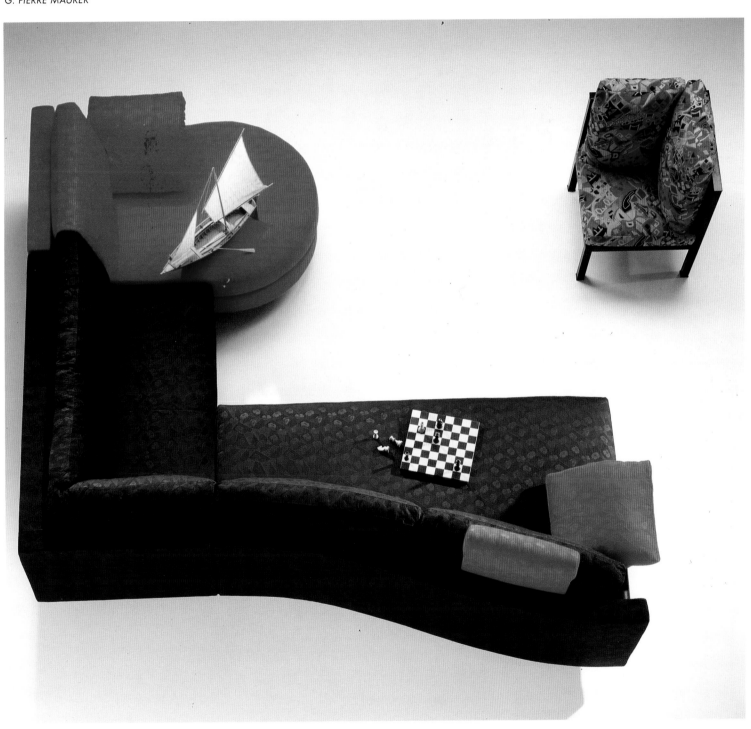

2
Tables
Desks
Carts

PRODUCT
ST. ANN'S SIDE TABLE
DESIGNER
CHRISTOPHER ROSE
FIRM
PEARL DOT LTD., ENGLAND
MANUFACTURER
PEARL DOT LTD., ENGLAND
DESCRIPTION
SYCAMORE, EBONY AND NICKEL SIDETABLE
PHOTO
JONATHAN TICKNER
DISTRIBUTOR
TIM WELLS FURNITURE

PRODUCT
AUBINTABLE (BEAST COLLECTION)
DESIGNER
DAVID SHAW NICHOLLS
FIRM
DAVID SHAW NICHOLLS CORP.
DISTRIBUTOR
MODERN AGE

PRODUCT
"CON TORTIONIST"
DESIGNER
LAURA JOHNSON
DESCRIPTION
*CAST ALUMINUM &
LACQUERED WOOD TABLE*
CLIENT
*AVAILABLE THROUGH ART
ET INDUSTRIE*
PHOTO
J. COSCIA JR.

PRODUCT
"YOU'D WARP TOO"
DESIGNER
PAUL LUDICK
DESCRIPTION
*MAPLE AND MAHOGANY
TABLES*
CLIENT
*AVAILABLE THROUGH ART
ET INDUSTRIE*
PHOTO
JOSEPH COSCIA, JR.

PRODUCT
BOW LEGGED TABLE
DESIGNER
FREDERIC SCHWARTZ
MANUFACTURER
SFA/LEINOFF
CLIENT
ASA
PHOTO
ELLIOT KAUFMAN

PRODUCT
CROCKTAIL TABLE
DESIGNER
MICHAEL WOLK
FIRM
MICHAEL WOLK DESIGN
ASSOCIATES
MANUFACTURER
MARTELL CO.
DESCRIPTION
LACQUERED POPLAR BASE
WITH A GLASS TOP
PHOTO
DAN FORER

PRODUCT
SIDE TABLES
DESIGNER
TIM WELLS
FIRM
FRED BAIER AND TIM
WELLS PARTNERSHIP
MANUFACTURER
TIM WELLS, THE PRESSURE
GROUP
DESCRIPTION
PAIR OF SMALL SIDE
TABLES; PRE-STAINED
VENEERS AND SOLID
MAPLE
PHOTO
DAVID MOHNEY
DISTRIBUTOR
TIM WELLS FURNITURE

PRODUCT
ROUNDED TRIANGLE
FORM COCKTAIL TABLE
DESIGNER
ALAN S. KUSHNER
DESCRIPTION
SILK-SCREEN TOP
PHOTO
ALICE SEBRELL

73

PRODUCT
BANNER TABLE
DESIGNER
GUIDO RODRIGUEZ
DESCRIPTION
*PAINTED WOOD AND
BRUSHED ALUMINUM BASE
WITH A GLASS TOP*
CLIENT
*AVAILABLE THROUGH
FULLSCALE*

PRODUCT
CONSOLE
DESIGNER
RHEA ALEXANDER
DESCRIPTION
*RUSTED STEEL FRAME,
CRYSTAL HANDLES AND
GLASS TABLE TOP.
AVAILABLE THROUGH
FULLSCALE*

PRODUCT
TOM TOM TABLES
DESIGNER
JOHN ERIC BYERS
MANUFACTURER
JOHN ERIC BYERS
DESCRIPTION
*BASE-EBONIZED CHERRY;
TOPS—VARIOUS WOOD
VENEERS (BLACK AND
WHITE PRINT)*
CLIENT
LIMITED PRODUCTION
PHOTO
TOM BRUMMETT

PRODUCT
POISE DINING TABLE
DESIGNER
GREGORY HIGGINS
MANUFACTURER
GREGORY HIGGINS
PHOTO
RON SHIRLEY

PRODUCT
PLAINS
DESIGNER
GREGORY HIGGINS
MANUFACTURER
GREGORY HIGGINS
PHOTO
RON SHIRLEY

PRODUCT
ARIANNETABLE (BEAST COLLECTION)
DESIGNER
DAVID SHAW NICHOLLS
FIRM
DAVID SHAW NICHOLLS CORP.
DISTRIBUTOR
MODERN AGE

PRODUCT
ANGUS TABLE (BEAST COLLECTION)
DESIGNER
DAVID SHAW NICHOLLS
FIRM
DAVID SHAW NICHOLLS CORP.
DISTRIBUTOR
MODERN AGE

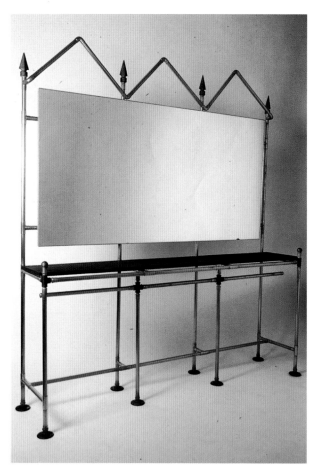

PRODUCT
GALAHAD CONSOLE
DESIGNER
BABETTE HOLLAND
MANUFACTURER
BABETTE HOLLAND
DESCRIPTION
*COPPER, CAST IRON, SLATE
AND MIRROR WITH
ALUMINUM TRIM*
CLIENT
*REPRESENTED BY
FURNITURE OF THE 20TH
CENTURY*

PRODUCT
DINING TABLE
DESIGNER
SUSAN MARYA FLORES
DESCRIPTION
STEEL AND GLASS TABLE
CLIENT
*REPRESENTED BY
FURNITURE OF THE 20TH
CENTURY*

PRODUCT
"TO CONTEMPLATE THE NEXT MOVE/ COUNTERPOINT SANCTUARY" COFFEE TABLE
DESIGNER
DAVID MOCARSKI
FIRM
TACTION DESIGN
CLIENT
MR. & MRS. ARNOLD FAMILIAN
PHOTO
CHARLES IMSTEPF

PRODUCT
LITTLE TIGER
DESIGNER
ALEXIS DE LA FALAISE
DESCRIPTION
SMALL SIDE TABLE WITH INLAYS.
CLIENT
U.S. REPRESENTATIVE— SARA VASS

PRODUCT
AUTUMN MOON
DESIGNER
NORMAN CAMPBELL
DESCRIPTION
WOOD, STEEL, GOLD LEAF AND STONE TABLE
CLIENT
AVAILABLE THROUGH ART ET INDUSTRIE
PHOTO
JOSEPH COSCIA, JR.

PRODUCT
"OF THE FUTURE/TAKE A STAND" COFFEE TABLE
DESIGNER
DAVID MOCARSKI
FIRM
TACTION DESIGN
CLIENT
ELAINE JOHNSON
PHOTO
CHARLES IMSTEPF

PRODUCT
MOTO
DESIGNER
RICHARD SNYDER
DESCRIPTION
*GLASS, HAND-PAINTED
ALUMINUM AND STEEL
TABLE*
CLIENT
ART ET INDUSTRIE
PHOTO
JOE COSCIA

PRODUCT
DELBANCO TABLE
DESIGNER
KURT B. DELBANCO
DESCRIPTION
GLASS TOP TABLE WOOD
BASE TOP & LEGS
PHOTO
JOHN SCHWARTZ

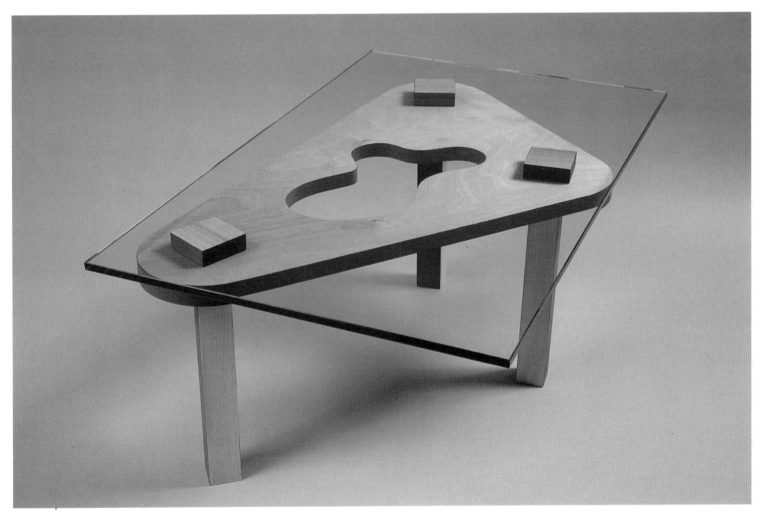

PRODUCT
DELTA BASE
CLIENT
GEO INTERNATIONAL

PRODUCT
*"IN-L" (CLOSE-UP OF
DETAIL)*
DESIGNER
ALLEN MIESNER
FIRM
MIESNER DESIGN

PRODUCT
"IN-L" (FULL VIEW)
DESIGNER
ALLEN MIESNER
FIRM
MIESNER DESIGN

PRODUCT
*CONNECTING VI DINING
TABLE*
DESIGNER
*STANLEY WEKSLER
CASSELMAN*
FIRM
*CASSELGLASS
INTERNATIONAL*
DESCRIPTION
*CONSTRUCTED WITH
GREEN MONOLITH
GLASS™*

PRODUCT
CITIES TABLE COLLECTION
DESIGNER
AL GLASS
FIRM
BECKER DESIGNED, INC.
MANUFACTURER
BECKER DESIGNED, INC.
DESCRIPTION
*CORDOVAN-STAINED
CHERRY AND STEEL*
PHOTO
LEN RIZZI

PRODUCT
MOSAIC TABLE
DESIGNER
SAM SOKOLOV
PHOTO
JOEL SOKOLOV

PRODUCT
GALAXY TABLE
DESIGNER
IRIS DeMAURO
FIRM
GEO INTERNATIONAL
CLIENT
GEO INTERNATIONAL
PHOTOGRAPHY
VICTOR SCHRAGER

PRODUCT
COFFEE TABLE
DESIGNER
PAMELA SLASS
DESCRIPTION
STEEL FRAME WITH A SILKSCREENED SLATE TABLE TOP
CLIENT
AVAILABLE THROUGH FULLSCALE

PRODUCT
MERIDIAN
DESIGNER
JAMES HONG
DESCRIPTION
LACQUERED STEEL AND GLASS TABLE
CLIENT
AVAILABLE THROUGH ART ET INDUSTRIE
PHOTO
JOSEPH COSCIA. JR.

PRODUCT
COMME SES CHEVEUX
DESIGNER
DAVID PALESCHUCK
DESCRIPTION
*BRUSHED AND ANODIZED
ALUMINUM WITH PURPLE
HEART WOOD TOP*
CLIENT
*AVAILABLE THROUGH
FULLSCALE*
PHOTO
F. STOPP

PRODUCT
SHAY TABLE
DESIGNER
DAVID PALESCHUCK
DESCRIPTION
*TEXTURED PAINTED STEEL
BASE WITH JITTERBUGGED
AND ANODIZED
ALUMINUM TOP. SIGNED
AND NUMBERED EDITION
LIMITED TO 100*
CLIENT
*AVAILABLE THROUGH
FULLSCALE*
PHOTO
PEDRO RIBA

PRODUCT
MARIMBA TABLE
DESIGNER
TOM FREEDMAN
FIRM
CUTTING EDGE
MANUFACTURER
CUTTING EDGE
PHOTO
DAVID L. BROWN

PRODUCT
LOUISA TABLE
DESIGNER
ALEXIS DE LA FALAISE
DESCRIPTION
*SMALL SIDE TABLE WITH
DRAWER.*
CLIENT
*U.S. REPRESENTATIVE—
SARA VASS*

PRODUCT
GREEN DESK
DESIGNER
BETH YOE
FIRM
CUTTING EDGE
MANUFACTURER
CUTTING EDGE
PHOTOGRAPHY
TOM FREEDMAN

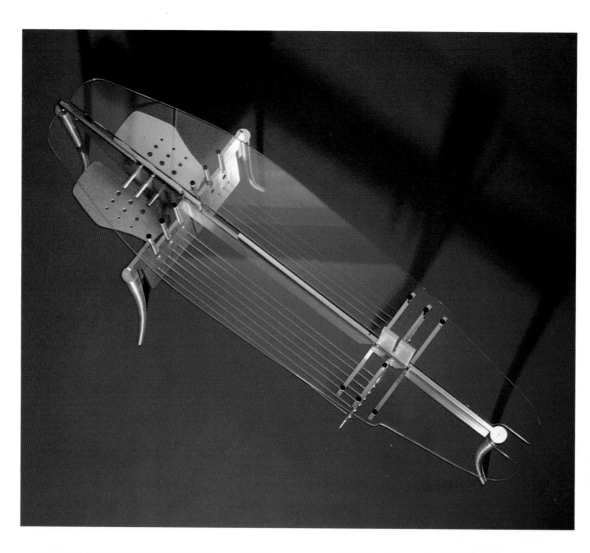

PRODUCT
CHRONZON TABLE
DESIGNERS
ALEX AMINI
JOHN BECKMANN
MANUFACTURER
AXIS MUNDI
PHOTO
SIMON FELDMAN

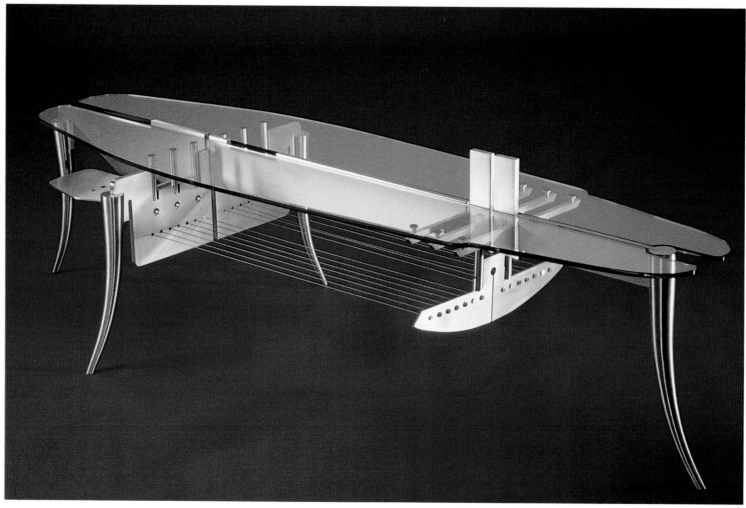

PRODUCT
DEMI-LUNE TABLE
DESIGNER
TOM FREEDMAN
FIRM
CUTTING EDGE
MANUFACTURER
CUTTING EDGE
PHOTO
DAVID L. BROWN

PRODUCT
*KOHOUTEK TRIANGLE
TABLE*
DESIGNER
LORELEI HÄMM
PHOTO
BILL DeMICHELE

PRODUCT
SLUGGER
DESIGNER
CARMEN SPERA
DESCRIPTION
*TABLE OF WOOD AND
GLASS*
CLIENT
*AVAILABLE THROUGH ART
ET INDUSTRIE*
PHOTO
JOSEPH COSCIA, JR.

PRODUCT
*"SKINNY LEGS" TABLE &
"SUMMER CHAIR"*
DESIGNER
ALLEN MIESNER
FIRM
MIESNER DESIGN

PRODUCT
TELEMATIC LANDSCAPE
(ELECTRONIC DESK)
(DETAIL OF TOP CORNER)
DESIGNER
PETER STATHIS
PHOTO
KEN SKALSKI

PRODUCT
TELEMATIC LANDSCAPE
(ELECTRONIC DESK)
(DETAIL OF BOTTOM
CORNER)
DESIGNER
PETER STATHIS
PHOTO
KEN SKALSKI

PRODUCT
PEDIMENT SERIES
DESIGNER
SHELTON MINDEL
MANUFACTURER
*LUTEN CLAREY STERN
CORP.*
PHOTO
JOHN BIGELOW TAYLOR

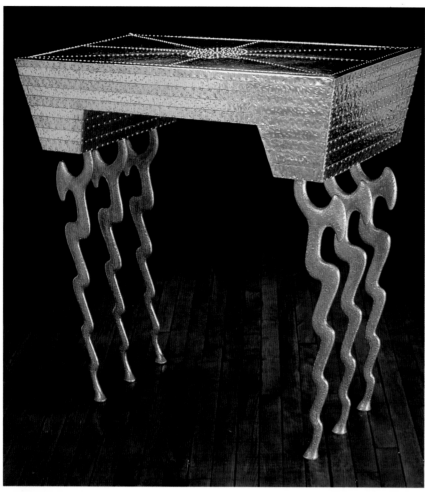

PRODUCT
*CONSOLE (FROM OTEKO
COLLECTION)*
DESIGNER
PETER DIEPENBROCK
MANUFACTURER
PETER DIEPENBROCK
PHOTO
JAMES BEARDS

PRODUCT
*"COBALT SERIES—
DELINEATION IN STEEL"
UNICONE END TABLE*
DESIGNER
PETER DIEPENBROCK
MANUFACTURER
PETER DIEPENBROCK
PHOTO
JAMES BEARDS

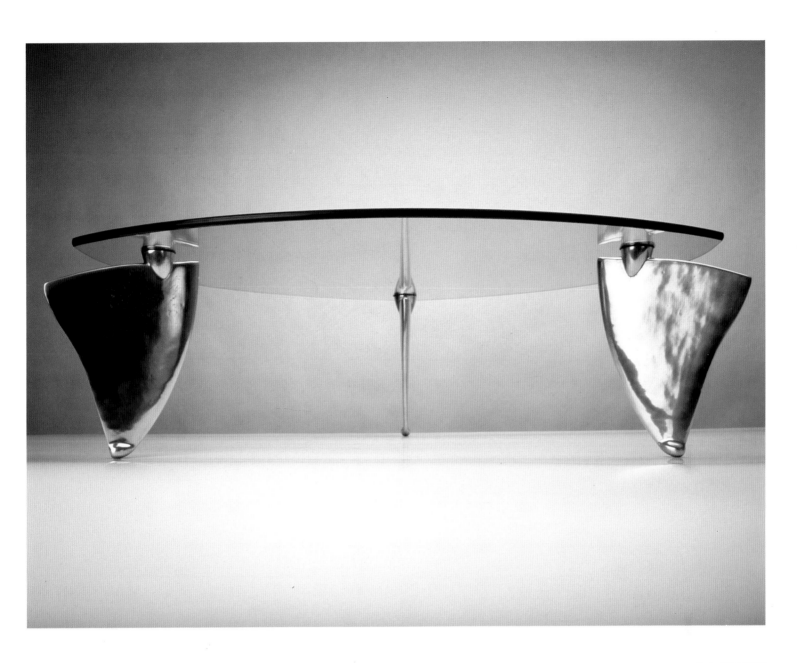

PRODUCT
FLIPPER TABLE
DESIGNER
MATTHEW HILTON
MANUFACTURER
PALAZZETTI

PRODUCT
TOVAGLIA TABLE 1989
DESIGNER
DAVIDE MERCATALI
DESCRIPTION
*CONSTRUCTED OF
NATURAL STEEL AND A
YELLOW ZINC METALLIZED*
CLIENT
METALS
PHOTO
SERGIO MERLI

PRODUCT
SALONNA TABLE
DESIGNER
PETER CARLSON
MANUFACTURER
LUTEN CLAREY STERN CORP.
PHOTO
JOHN BIGELOW TAYLOR

PRODUCT
211 CONSOLE
DESIGNER
GUIDO RODRIGUEZ
DESCRIPTION
*PLUM PATINATED STEEL
FRAME WITH
JITTERBUGGED ALUMINUM
TOP. SIGNED AND
NUMBERED LIMITED
EDITION OF 100*
CLIENT
*AVAILABLE THROUGH
FULLSCALE*
PHOTO
PEDRO RIBA

PRODUCT
SHAY COFFEE TABLE
DESIGNER
DAVID PALESCHUCK
DESCRIPTION
*TEXTURED PAINTED STEEL
BASE WITH JITTERBUGGED
AND ANODIZED
ALUMINUM TOP. SIGNED
AND NUMBERED LIMITED
EDITION OF 100*
CLIENT
*AVAILABLE THROUGH
FULLSCALE*
PHOTO
PEDRO RIBA

PRODUCT
LINIAL
DESIGNER
HELLE DAMKJAER
MANUFACTURER
QUARTELT, GERMANY
PHOTO
SANDRO LAURENZO

PRODUCT
*DOUBLE DIAMOND
STICKPIN*
DESIGNER
CARMEN SPERA
DESCRIPTION
*GLASS, COPPER, WOOD
AND PIGMENT TABLE*
CLIENT
*AVAILABLE THROUGH ART
ET INDUSTRIE*
PHOTO
JOSEPH COSCIA, JR.

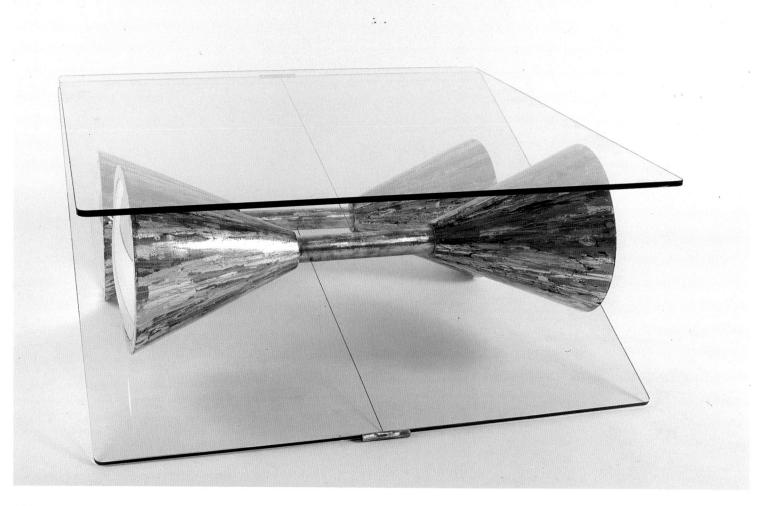

PRODUCT
"COBALT SERIES—
DELINEATIONS IN STEEL"
(END TABLE)
DESIGNER
PETER DIEPENBROCK
MANUFACTURER
PETER DIEPENBROCK
PHOTO
JAMES BEARDS

PRODUCT
CONSOLE
DESIGNER
GUIDO RODRIGUEZ
DESCRIPTION
ALUMINUM BASE WITH A
COBALT BLUE GLASS TOP
CLIENT
AVAILABLE THROUGH
FULLSCALE

PRODUCT
COFFEE TABLE
DESIGNER
IRIS FINGERHUT
DESCRIPTION
*CARVED JELUTONG
WOOD, GLASS AND DEER
ANTLER*
PHOTO
NICOLE KATANO

PRODUCT
SERIES APPIA TABLE
DESIGNER
RICHARD LEIBOWITZ
DESCRIPTION
*PICKLED OAK WITH BRASS
AND A GLASS TOP*
CLIENT
*AVAILABLE THROUGH
FULLSCALE*

PRODUCT
COCKTAIL TABLE
DESIGNER
ALAN S. KUSHNER
DESCRIPTION
*ROUNDED TRIANGLE
FORM SILK SCREEN TOP-
STAINED BUTTERNUT-
GLASS TOP 64 × 32*
PHOTO
ALICE SEBRELL

PRODUCT
WEDDING TABLE
DESIGNER
RICHARD SNYDER
FIRM
RICHARD SNYDER DESIGN
DESCRIPTION
SIDEBOARD WITH CURVED
MAHOGANY TOP AND
TURNED LEGS
CLIENT
AVAILABLE THROUGH ART
ET INDUSTRIE
PHOTO
JOE COSCIA

PRODUCT
END TABLE (#2)
DESIGNER
BETH FORER
MANUFACTURER
CESAR CABRAL, BETH
FORER
DESCRIPTION
FURNITURE CONSTRUCTED
OF HANDMADE TILES ON
WOOD. DECORATED BY
MISHIMA TECHNIQUE—
COLORED CLAY INLAID
WITH CONTRASTING SLIP,
UNDER A CLEAR GLAZE
PHOTO
BETH FORER

PRODUCT
BLOOM TABLE
DESIGNER
JAMES VAN ETTEN

PRODUCT
DIANE
DESIGNER
ALEXIS DE LA FALAISE
DESCRIPTION
TABLE-CONSOLE
CLIENT
*U.S. REPRESENTATIVE—
SARA VASS*

PRODUCT
*"IL TAVOLO PER ALDO"
TABLE (TOP VIEW)*
DESIGNER
SHIGERU UCHIDA
FIRM
STUDIO 80
MANUFACTURER
CHAIRS
DESCRIPTION
*MADE FROM BIRCH
PLYWOOD WITH PEBBLE
FINISH, LEGS OF (CHERRY)
WOOD ADJUSTABLE
WORM SCREWS*
PHOTO
NACÁSA & PARTNERS INC.

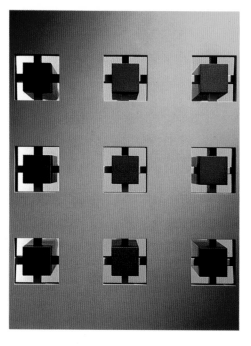

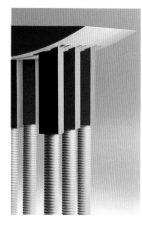

PRODUCT
*"IL TAVOLO PER ALDO"
TABLE (DETAIL)*
DESIGNER
SHIGERU UCHIDA
FIRM
STUDIO 80
MANUFACTURER
CHAIRS
DESCRIPTION
*MADE OF BIRCH
PLYWOOD WITH PEBBLE
FINISH, LEGS OF (CHERRY)
WOOD ADJUSTABLE
WORM SCREWS*
PHOTO
NACÁSA & PARTNERS INC.

PRODUCT
TABLE
DESIGNER
DAVID PERRY
DESCRIPTION
MAHOGANY, COPPERLEAF
WITH PATINA
PHOTO
SUSAN EINSTEIN

PRODUCT
STAR TREK TABLE
DESIGNER
JOEL SOKOLOV
PHOTO
JOEL SOKOLOV

PRODUCT
LIGHT/STORAGE CUBES
AND "MOTHER" TABLES
WITH TRAYS
DESIGNER
JOEL SOKOLOV
PHOTO
JOEL SOKOLOV

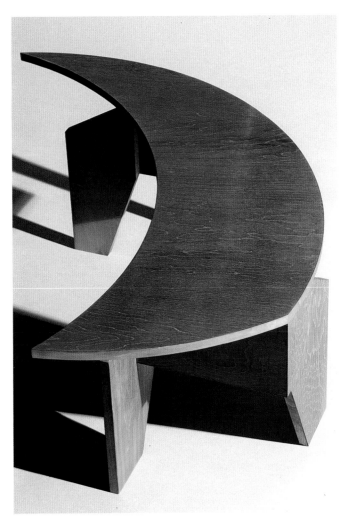

PRODUCT
*CHAMELEON COFFEE
TABLE*
DESIGNER
LEO J. BLACKMAN
MANUFACTURER
JOHN GONZALEZ
DESCRIPTION
*ANALINE-DYED PLYWOOD
TABLE. COMES IN A SET
OF 3.*
PHOTO
RICHARD HACKETT

PRODUCT
TRIO TABLES
DESIGNER
LEO J. BLACKMAN
MANUFACTURER
JOHN GONZALEZ
DESCRIPTION
*3 DIAMOND SHAPED
TABLES THAT CAN BE
CONFIGURED INTO A
MYRIAD OF SHAPES*
PHOTO
RICHARD HACKETT

PRODUCT
MIAMI WAVES TABLE
DESIGNER
MICHAEL WOLK
FIRM
*MICHAEL WOLK DESIGN
ASSOCIATES*
MANUFACTURER
STANSSON STUDIO
DESCRIPTION
*PAINTED ALUMINUM BASE
WITH A ¾"-THICK GLASS
TOP*
AWARD
*MIAMI STYLE FURNITURE
DESIGN COMPETITION,
1988—2ND PLACE—
OVERALL*

PRODUCT
EQUIPOISE
DESIGNER
GREGORY HIGGINS
MANUFACTURER
GREGORY HIGGINS
PHOTO
RON SHIRLEY

PRODUCT
CITIES TABLE COLLECTION
DESIGNER
AL GLASS
FIRM
BECKER DESIGNED, INC.
MANUFACTURER
BECKER DESIGNED, INC.
DESCRIPTION
*CORDOVAN STAINED
CHERRY AND STEEL;
WHITEWASHED MAPLE
AND STEEL*
PHOTO
LEN RIZZI

PRODUCT
DROP LEAF TABLE
DESIGNER
DALE BROHOLM
MANUFACTURER
DALE BROHOLM
PHOTO
POWELL PHOTOGRAPHY

PRODUCT
CUT OUTS DINING TABLE
DESIGNER
LLOYD SCHWAN
FIRM
GODLEY-SCHWAN
PHOTO
JOHN DeLUCA

PRODUCT
*ST. ANN'S DIRECTIONAL
TABLE*
DESIGNER
CHRISTOPHER ROSE
FIRM
PEARL DOT LTD., ENGLAND
MANUFACTURER
PEARL DOT LTD., ENGLAND
DESCRIPTION
*USUALLY IN ASH, OAK OR
SYCAMORE. VENEERED
TOP WITH SOLID ROLLED
EDGES AND DETACHABLE
LEG FRAMES*
DISTRIBUTOR
TIM WELLS FURNITURE

PRODUCT
*JUGENDSTIL COLLECTION
(ROUND TABLE & CHAIRS)*
DESIGNER
BERND MÜNZEBROCK
MANUFACTURER
GEIGER INT'L
CLIENT
GEIGER INT'L

PRODUCT
TABLE
DESIGNER
DAVID PERRY
DESCRIPTION
SYCAMORE AND WENGE
PHOTO
SUSAN EINSTEIN

PRODUCT
*JUGENDSTIL COLLECTION
(CONF. TABLE & CHAIRS)*
DESIGNER
BERND MÜNZEBROCK
MANUFACTURER
GEIGER INT'L
CLIENT
GEIGER INT'L

PRODUCT
GERTRUDE & ALICE TABLES
(2 PIECES)
DESIGNER
LEO J. BLACKMAN
MANUFACTURER
JOHN GONZALEZ
CLIENT
LEO J. BLACKMAN
PHOTO
RICHARD HACKETT

PRODUCT
TRIUNA COLLECTION
FIRM
GEIGER INTERNATIONAL
DESCRIPTION
A COLLECTION OF TABLES.
CLIENT
FOR MORE INFORMATION:
WILLIAM KENT
SCHOENFISCH

PRODUCT
GERTRUDE & ALICE TABLES
(WHOLE SYSTEM)
DESIGNER
LEO J. BLACKMAN
MANUFACTURER
JOHN GONZALEZ
CLIENT
LEO J. BLACKMAN
PHOTO
RICHARD HACKETT

PRODUCT
MANDARIN TABLE
DESIGNER
STANLEY JAY FRIEDMAN
MANUFACTURER
BRUETON INDUSTRIES
AWARD
1988 ROSCOE AWARD

PRODUCT
*"SEARCHING FOR BREATH/
PASSING IN THE NITE"
ENTRY TABLE*
DESIGNER
DAVID MOCARSKI
FIRM
TACTION DESIGN
PHOTO
CHARLES IMSTEPF

PRODUCT
DESK
DESIGNER
DAVID PERRY
DESCRIPTION
*MAPLE AND SANDED
COLORCORE*
PHOTO
FOUR EYES

PRODUCT
*ARQUITECTURA TABLE &
LAMP*
DESIGNER
*SERGIO OROZCO FOR
BRUETON INDUSTRIES*
MANUFACTURER
BRUETON INDUSTRIES
AWARD
1989 ROSCOE AWARD

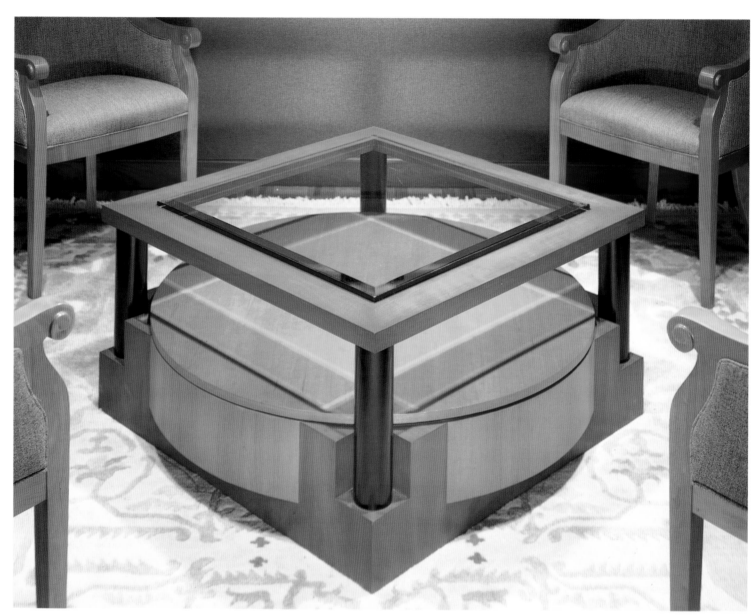

PRODUCT
AUGUST POLIG TABLE
DESIGNER
MICHAEL WOLK
FIRM
MICHAEL WOLK DESIGN
ASSOCIATES
MANUFACTURER
MARTELL CO.
DESCRIPTION
CHERRY BASE WITH A ¾"-
THICK CLEAR GLASS TOP
PHOTO
MARK ROSCUMS

PRODUCT
BREAKERS CONSOLE
DESIGNER
*SIRMOS, A DIVISION OF
BROMANTE CORPORATION*
FIRM
*SIRMOS, A DIVISION OF
BROMANTE CORPORATION*
MANUFACTURER
SIRMOS
DESCRIPTION
*VERMONT MARBLE TOP
WITH CLASSICALLY
INSPIRED LAUREL LEAF
AND GARLAND MOTIFS*
PHOTO
SIRMOS

PRODUCT
TRIANON CENTRE TABLE
DESIGNER
*SIRMOS, A DIVISION OF
BROMANTE CORPORATION*
FIRM
*SIRMAS, A DIVISION OF
BROMANTE CORPORATION*
MANUFACTURER
*SIRMOS, A DIVISION OF
BROMANTE CORP.*
DESCRIPTION
*INSPIRED BY FRENCH
REGENCY PERIOD*
PHOTO
DURSTON SAYLOR
AWARD
ROSCOE AWARD

PRODUCT
VANITY AND MIRROR
DESIGNER
IRIS FINGERHUT
DESCRIPTION
*CARVED JELUTONG
WOOD, GOLD LEAF,
WROUGHT IRON, LEATHER
TOP*
PHOTO
NICOLE KATANO

PRODUCT
WRITING TABLE AND CHAIR
DESIGNER
IRIS FINGERHUT
DESCRIPTION
CARVED JELUTONG WOOD, GOLD LEAF, WROUGHT IRON, LEATHER TOP
PHOTO
NICOLE KATANO

PRODUCT
UFO TABLE
DESIGNER
DON RUDDY

PRODUCT
BAR CART
DESIGNER
ENZO MARI
MANUFACTURER
ALESSI
CLIENT
MARKUSE CORP.

PRODUCT
CHAIR AND TABLE
DESIGNER
DAVID PERRY
DESCRIPTION
PINE, ASH, LACQUER
PHOTO
SUSAN EINSTEIN

PRODUCT
LUNA CART
TWILIGHT TABLE
DESIGNER
DON RUDDY

PRODUCT
PLANTER
TWILIGHT TABLE
DESIGNER
DON RUDDY

PRODUCT
SIDE TABLE
DESIGNER
IRIS FINGERHUT
DESCRIPTION
*ASH, SILVER AND LAPIS
LAZULI INLAY, SILVER
DRAWER PULL WITH SEMI-
PRECIOUS STONES*
PHOTO
NICOLE KATANO

PRODUCT
SMALL MAHOGANY TABLE
DESIGNER
IRIS FINGERHUT
DESCRIPTION
*MAHOGANY, BRASS
RINGS, ANTIQUE BEADS*
PHOTO
NICOLE KATANO

3

Chests
Cabinets
Sideboards

PRODUCT
CITI CABINET #3
DESIGNER
JOEL SOKOLOV
PHOTO
JOEL SOKOLOV

PRODUCT
WALL CABINET
DESIGNER
TOM FREEDMAN
FIRM
CUTTING EDGE
MANUFACTURER
CUTTING EDGE
PHOTO
TOM FREEDMAN

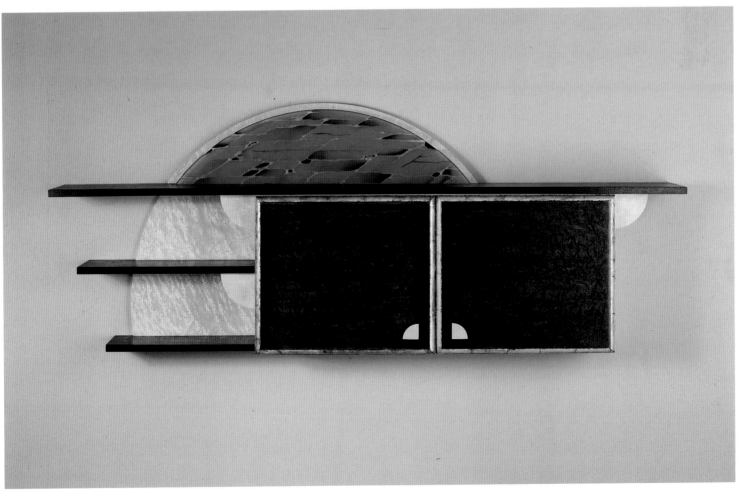

PRODUCT
CITI CABINET #3
DESIGNER
PHOTO
JOEL SOKOLOV

PRODUCT
*TROPIC VIDEO/AUDIO
CABINET WITH LIGHT/
SPEAKERS BOX*
DESIGNER
JOEL SOKOLOV
DESCRIPTION
PHOTO
JOEL SOKOLOV

PRODUCT
ASTONSIDEBOARD (BEAST COLLECTION)
DESIGNER
DAVID SHAW NICHOLLS
FIRM
DAVID SHAW NICHOLLS CORP.
DISTRIBUTOR
MODERN AGE

PRODUCT
CABINET OF FOUR WISHES
DESIGNER
RICHARD SNYDER
FIRM
RICHARD SNYDER DESIGN
DESCRIPTION
A ROUGHLY-TEXTURED ANCIENT-LOOKING CHEST OF DRAWERS, IN LACQUERED MAHOGANY WITH BRASS
CLIENT
AVAILABLE THROUGH ART ET INDUSTRIE
PHOTOGRAPHY
BILL WHITE

135

PRODUCT
SARONG CABINET
DESIGNER
RICHARD SNYDER
DESCRIPTION
WOOD & PIGMENT
CLIENT
*AVAILABLE THROUGH ART
ET INDUSTRIE*
PHOTO
JOE COSCIA

PRODUCT
BLANKET CHEST (DETAIL)
DESIGNER
BETH FORER
MANUFACTURER
CESAR CABRAL,
BETH FORER
DESCRIPTION
FURNITURE CONSTRUCTED
OF HANDMADE TILES ON
WOOD. DECORATED BY
MISHIMA TECHNIQUE—
COLORED CLAY INLAID
WITH CONTRASTING SLIP,
UNDER A CLEAR GLAZE
PHOTO
BETH FORER

PRODUCT
*CITISCAPE-WALL CABINET/
BAR*
DESIGNER
JOEL SOKOLOV
DESCRIPTION
PHOTO
JOEL SOKOLOV

PRODUCT
THEY DANCE ALONE AT NIGHT
DESIGNER
RICHARD SNYDER
DESCRIPTION
SACRED PIGMENT, TAR AND WOOD FROM THE CENTER OF THE FOREST
CLIENT
AVAILABLE THROUGH ART ET INDUSTRIE
PHOTO
JOE COSCIA

PRODUCT
ONDA QUADRA
DESIGNER
MARIO BELLINI
FIRM
ATELIER INTERNATIONAL,
LTD.
MANUFACTURER
ATELIER INTERNATIONAL,
LTD.
DESCRIPTION
STACKED STORAGE UNITS
PHOTO
STUDIO PHOTOGRAPHERS
IN ITALY

PRODUCT
*CABINET OF THE 7
MOSQUES*
DESIGNER
RICHARD SNYDER
DESCRIPTION
*PAINTED WOOD AND
PRAYER SOUNDS*
CLIENT
*AVAILABLE THROUGH ART
ET INDUSTRIE*
PHOTO
BILL WHITE

PRODUCT
BEGGAR'S BOWL
DESIGNER
RICHARD SNYDER
DESCRIPTION
*CARVED WOOD, PIGMENT
AND ROPE*
CLIENT
*AVAILABLE THROUGH ART
ET INDUSTRIE*
PHOTO
JOE COSCIA

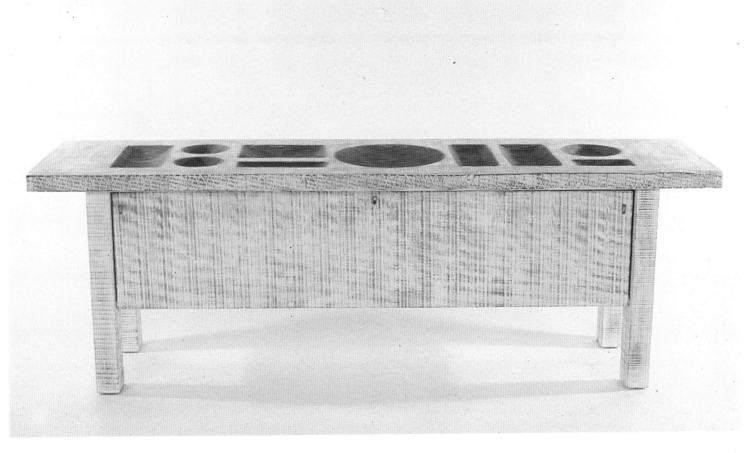

PRODUCT
THE CHICAGO BUFFET
DESIGNER
ALAN S. KUSHNER
MANUFACTURER
ALAN S. KUSHNER
DESCRIPTION
*BUFFET COMPOSED OF
STAINED ASH WITH A
MARBLE INSET TOP. DOORS
ARE COMPOSED OF
STAINED ASH FRAMES
WITH BIRDSEYE MAPLE
PANELS. WOOD DETAILS
ARE ASH AND WALNUT.*
PHOTO
KAREN MAUCH

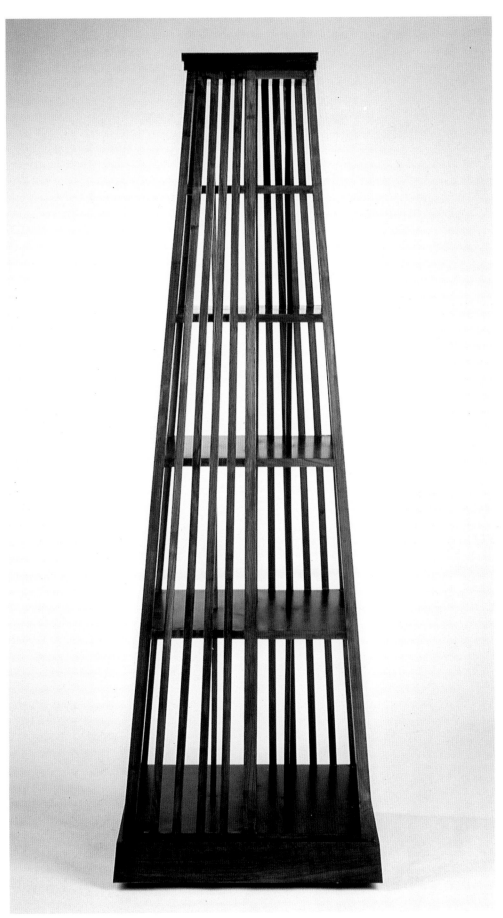

PRODUCT
RAYON DE SOLEIL
DESIGNER
ALEXIS DE LA FALAISE
DESCRIPTION
ETAGERE (BOOKCASE) IN WALNUT, WAXED OAK, NATURAL SYCAMORE AND TINTED "EBONY."
CLIENT
U.S. REPRESENTATIVE— SARA VASS

143

PRODUCT
"L'ARMADIO PER ALDO"
CABINET (DETAIL)
DESIGNER
SHIGERU UCHIDA
FIRM
STUDIO 80
MANUFACTURER
CHAIRS
DESCRIPTION
MADE OF BIRCH
PLYWOOD W/ PEBBLE
FINISH LEGS OF (CHERRY)
WOOD ADJUSTABLE
WORM SCREWS
PHOTO
NACÁSA & PARTNERS INC.

PRODUCT
"L'ARMADIO PER ALDO"
CABINET
DESIGNER
SHIGERU UCHIDA
FIRM
STUDIO 80
MANUFACTURER
CHAIRS
DESCRIPTION
MADE OF BIRCH
PLYWOOD WITH PEBBLE
FINISH; LEGS OF CHERRY
WOOD WITH ADJUSTABLE
WORM SCREWS
PHOTO
NACÁSA & PARTNERS INC.

PRODUCT
TV CABINET (OPEN)
DESIGNER
JOEL SOKOLOV

PRODUCT
TV CABINET (CLOSED)
DESIGNER
JOEL SOKOLOV

PRODUCT
3 UNITS
DESIGNER
JOEL SOKOLOV

PRODUCT
TV/STEREO CABINET
DESIGNER
JOHN ERIC BYERS
MANUFACTURER
JOHN ERIC BYERS
DESCRIPTION
CABINET ON ARCH
CLIENT
PRIVATE COLLECTION
PHOTO
TOM BRUMMETT

PRODUCT
THIN MAN CABINET
DESIGNER
LESTER EVAN TOUR, AIA

PRODUCT
TADAO
DESIGNER
ROBERTO LAZZERONI
FIRM
CECCOTTI COLLEZIONE
MANUFACTURER
CECCOTTI COLLEZIONE
DESCRIPTION
*OVOID-SHAPED
SIDEBOARD—SOLID
CHERRY WOOD OR
WALNUT WITH A WAX
FINISH, TWO DOORS AND
TWO DRAWERS; INTERNAL
PART OF DRAWERS AND
INTERNAL SHELVES IN
MAPLE AND PADAUK
RESPECTIVELY.*
CLIENT
CECCOTTI COLLEZIONE
PHOTOGRAPHY
MARIO CIAMPI
DISTRIBUTOR
FREDERIC WILLIAMS

PRODUCT
WEDGE (DESK) (OPEN)
DESIGNER
ALLEN MIESNER
FIRM
MIESNER DESIGN

PRODUCT
ONDA QUADRA
DESIGNER
MARIO BELLINI
FIRM
ATELIER INTERNATIONAL,
LTD.
MANUFACTURER
ATELIER INTERNATIONAL,
LTD.
DESCRIPTION
STACKED STORAGE UNITS
PHOTO
STUDIO PHOTOGRAPHERS
IN ITALY

PRODUCT
ONDA QUADRA
DESIGNER
MARIO BELLINI
FIRM
ATELIER INTERNATIONAL,
LTD.
MANUFACTURER
ATELIER INTERNATIONAL,
LTD.
DESCRIPTION
STACKED STORAGE UNITS
PHOTO
STUDIO PHOTOGRAPHERS
IN ITALY

149

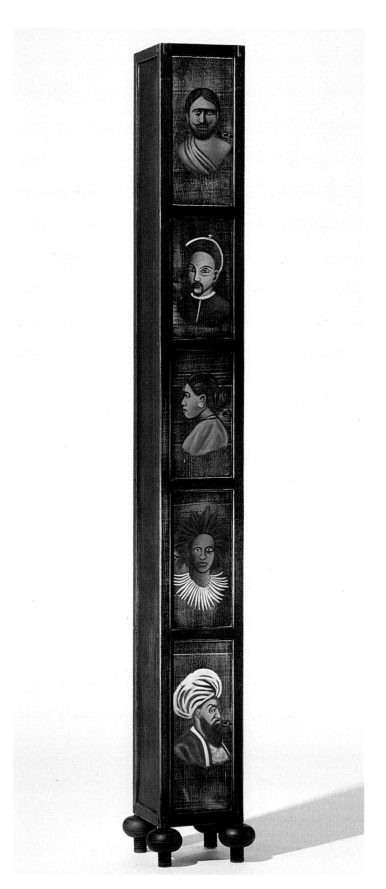

PRODUCT
*CABINET OF THE PEOPLE
WHO GOT LOST*
DESIGNER
RICHARD SNYDER
DESCRIPTION
*LACQUERED WOOD AND
PAINT*
CLIENT
*AVAILABLE THROUGH ART
ET INDUSTRIE*
PHOTO
JOE COSCIA

PRODUCT
CITI CABINET #3
DESIGNER
JOEL SOKOLOV
PHOTO
JOEL SOKOLOV

PRODUCT
DOWRY CHEST
DESIGNER
JOHN ERIC BYERS
MANUFACTURER
JOHN ERIC BYERS
DESCRIPTION
*EBONIZED OAK, ASH,
PATINATED COPPER RIVETS
(SIDE)*
CLIENT
PRIVATE COLLECTION
PHOTO
TOM BRUMMETT

PRODUCT
GB CABINET
DESIGNER
JOEL SOKOLOV

151

Shelving Units
Office Systems

PRODUCT
*"CONTRAPUNTO"
SHELVING (FULL VIEW
FROM RIGHT SIDE)*
DESIGNER
JAIME TRESSERRA
FIRM
J. TRESSERRA DESIGN S.L.

PRODUCT
CITY SHELF
DESIGNER
MICHAEL WOLK
FIRM
*MICHAEL WOLK DESIGN
ASSOCIATES*
MANUFACTURER
MARTELL CO.
DESCRIPTION
*MARBLE AND MAHOGANY
SHELVING UNIT*
PHOTO
NANCY WATSON

PRODUCT
HIFI SUPPORT
DESIGNER
PAUL BRADLEY
DESCRIPTION
MAPLE AND PURPLE HEART
CLIENT
OBJECT DESIGN
PHOTO
RICK ENGLISH

PRODUCT
SHELVING UNIT
DESIGNER
JOANNE McCOBB
DESCRIPTION
*NATURAL AND LAMINATED
CHERRY WITH ALUMINUM
SIDE PANELS*
CLIENT
*AVAILABLE THROUGH
FULLSCALE*

PRODUCT
CITISCAPE-LIVING UNIT
DESIGNER
JOEL SOKOLOV
DESCRIPTION
*SYSTEM IS COMPRISED OF
DESK, DRESSER, TV TABLE,
LIGHTS, CLOCK, SHELVING*
PHOTO
JOEL SOKOLOV

155

PRODUCT
*DOMUS CONTAINER
BASED FURNISHINGS
(BOOKCASES,
SHOWCASES, WALL
FITTINGS)*
DESIGNER
ANTONIO CITTERIO
MANUFACTURER
B & B ITALIA
PHOTO
ALDO BALLO

PRODUCT
DOMUS CONTAINER BASED FURNISHINGS (BOOKCASES, SHOWCASES, WALL FITTINGS)
DESIGNER
ANTONIO CITTERIO
MANUFACTURER
B & B ITALIA
PHOTO
ALDO BALLO

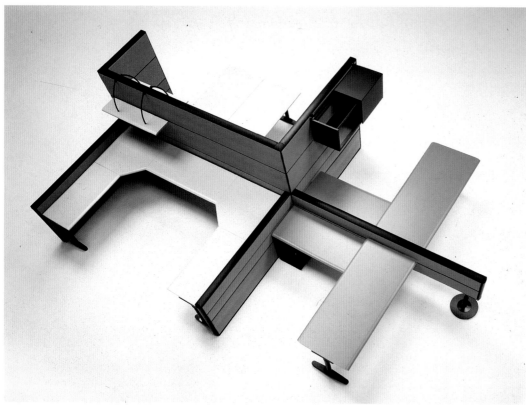

PRODUCT
ABAK (OFFICE PARTITIONS)
DESIGNER
STUDIO KAIROS
MANUFACTURER
B & B ITALIA
PHOTO
LUCIANO SOAVE

PRODUCT
TRAVAIL
DESIGNER
ALEXIS DE LA FALAISE
DESCRIPTION
DESK
CLIENT
*U.S. REPRESENTATIVE—
SARA VASS*

159

PRODUCT
*JUGENDSTIL COLLECTION
(TABLE, CHAIRS,
BOOKSHELF)*
DESIGNER
BERND MÜNZEBROCK
MANUFACTURER
GEIGER INT'L
CLIENT
GEIGER INT'L

PRODUCT
*FIRST WORLD DESK AND
WALL PIECE*
DESIGNER
JAMES EVANSON
DESCRIPTION
*LACQUERED WOOD,
COPPER, STEEL, AND
GLASS*
CLIENT
*AVAILABLE THROUGH ART
ET INDUSTRIE*
PHOTO
JOSEPH COSCIA, JR.

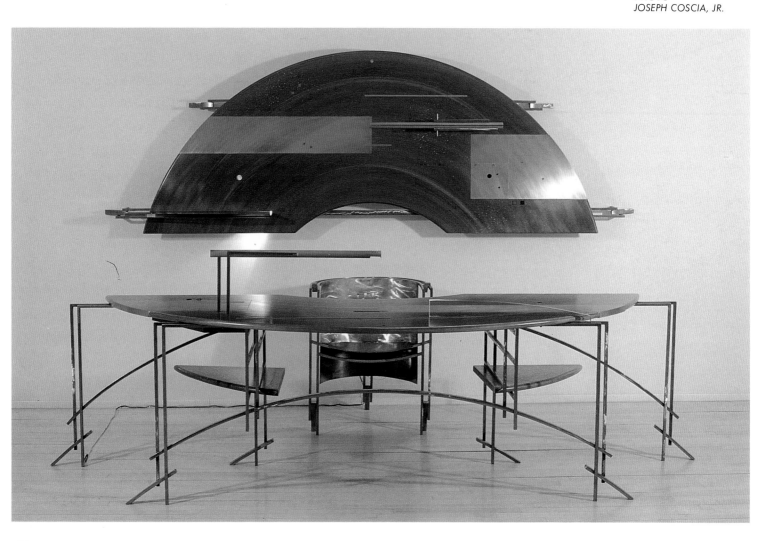

PRODUCT
TRIUNA COLLECTION
DESIGNER
MANFRED PETRI
MANUFACTURER
GEIGER INT'L
DESCRIPTION
DESK AND SIDEBOARD
CLIENT
GEIGER INT'L

PRODUCT
JUGENDSTIL COLLECTION
(TABLE & DESK & CHAIRS)
DESIGNER
BERND MÜNZEBROCK
MANUFACTURER
GEIGER INT'L
CLIENT
GEIGER INT'L

161

Lighting

PRODUCT
LIGHT TOWER
DESIGNER
MICHAEL WOLK
FIRM
MICHAEL WOLK DESIGN ASSOCIATES
MANUFACTURER
STANSSON STUDIO
DESCRIPTION
EXTRUDED ALUMINUM CASTING AND PLEXIGLASS, H.I.D. LAMP, POLISHED REFLECTOR
PHOTO
NANCY WATSON

PRODUCT
SNARE LIGHT
DESIGNER
FREDERIC SCHWARTZ
MARC L'ITALIAN
FIRM
ANDERSON/SCHWARTZ ARCHITECTS
MANUFACTURER
ASAP
PHOTO
ELLIOT KAUFMAN

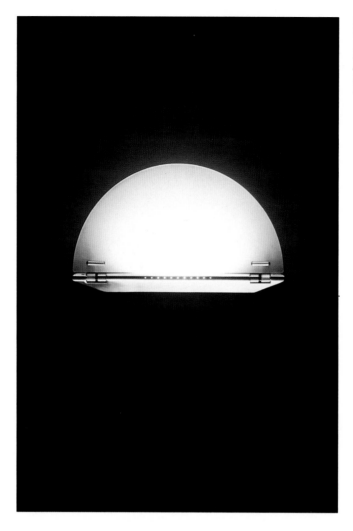

PRODUCT
VERTE A
DESIGNER
SERGE DEVESA
MANUFACTURER
*METALARTE FOR HANSEN
LAMPS*

PRODUCT
DAKOTA SCONCE
DESIGNER
JOSEP LLUSCA
MANUFACTURER
*METALARTE FOR HANSEN
LAMPS*

PRODUCT
"TRIA" SCONCE
DESIGNER
ANDRZEJ DULJAS
FIRM
KOCH & LOWY
MANUFACTURER
KOCH & LOWY
PHOTO
MARCUS TULLIS

PRODUCT
GRALL GAMMA SCONCE
DESIGNER
FLOS, INC.
MANUFACTURER
FLOS, INC.

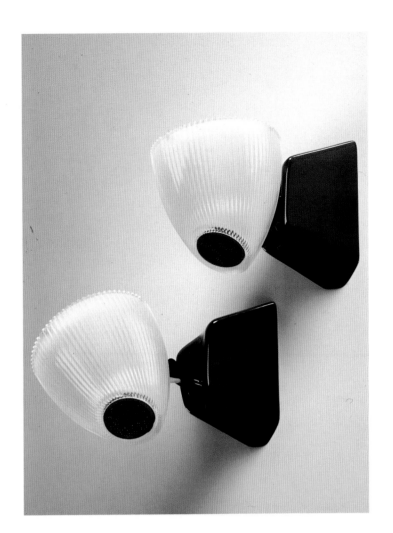

PRODUCT
ALUMINUM WALL SCONCE
DESIGNER
RICHARD LEIBOWITZ
DESCRIPTION
*ALUMINUM FRAME, KOCI
PAPER, FLUORESCENT
LIGHT SOURCE*
CLIENT
*AVAILABLE THROUGH
FULLSCALE*

PRODUCT
AL 480 WS
DESIGNER
APPLETON LAMPLIGHTER
MANUFACTURER
APPLETON LAMPLIGHTER
DESCRIPTION
*WALL SCONCE OF
ALUMINUM AND ACRYLIC*
CLIENT
APPLETON LAMPLIGHTER

PRODUCT
UFO SCONCE
DESIGNER
DON RUDDY

PRODUCT
THE FALL
DESIGNER
HOWARD MEISTER
DESCRIPTION
*HAND WROUGHT AND
PAINTED STEEL*
CLIENT
*AVAILABLE THROUGH ART
ET INDUSTRIE*
PHOTO
JOE COSCIA, JR.

PRODUCT
ARCANE SCONCE
DESIGNER
FELIPE MORALES
FIRM
GEO INT'L
CLIENT
GEO INT'L
PHOTO
VICTOR SCHRAGEN

PRODUCT
AURA
DESIGNER
*PERRY A. KING AND
SANTIAGO MIRANDA*
MANUFACTURER
*ATELIER INTERNATIONAL,
INC.*
DESCRIPTION
*WALL SCONCE COMPOSED
OF A WING-LIKE,
UPWARDLY CURVED STEEL
REFLECTOR*
CLIENT
*ATELIER INTERNATIONAL,
INC.*

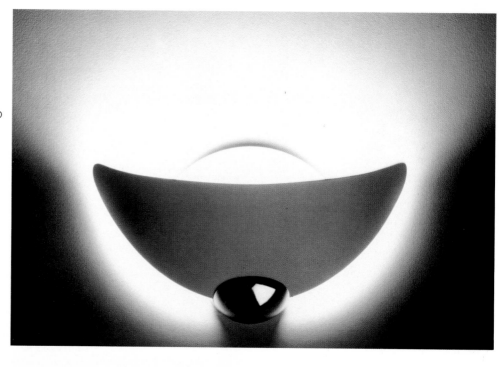

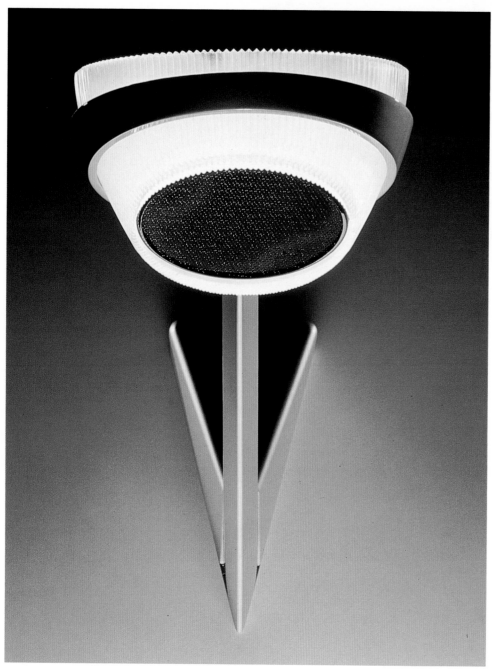

PRODUCT
GRALL SIGMA SCONCE
DESIGNER
*PAOLO FERRARI, LUCIANO
PAGANI AND ANGELO
PERRERSI ASSOCIATES*
MANUFACTURER
FLOS INC.
DESCRIPTION
*A LARGE-SCALE WALL
SCONCE CONSISTING OF
A FROSTED, RIBBED GLASS
DIFFUSER SECURED TO AN
EXTENDED METAL ARM
WITH A CAST-ALUMINUM
ALLOY RING*
CLIENT
FLOS INC.

PRODUCT
NOCE 3
DESIGNER
ACHILLE CASTIGLIONI
MANUFACTURER
FLOS INC.
DESCRIPTION
*A WALL MOUNTED
FIXTURE OF A FROSTED
CAST GLASS DIFFUSER
SECURED BY AN
ALUMINUM RING TO THE
DIE CAST ALUMINUM BASE*
CLIENT
FLOS INC.

PRODUCT
GRALL DELTA CS
DESIGN
*PAOLO FERRARI, LUCIANO
PAGANI AND ANGELO
PERVERSI ASSOCIATES*
MANUFACTURER
FLOS INC.
DESCRIPTION
*CEILING MOUNTED
SPOTLIGHT*
CLIENT
FLOS INC.

PRODUCT
*BERTILLE AP27632 WALL
SCONCE*
DESIGNER
ANDREE PUTMAN
MANUFACTURER
*BALDINGER
ARCHITECTURAL LIGHTING
INC.*

PRODUCT
*BERTILLE AP27632 WALL
SCONCE*
DESIGNER
ANDREE PUTMAN
MANUFACTURER
*BALDINGER
ARCHITECTURAL LIGHTING
INC.*

PRODUCT
*VICTORIE AP27633 WALL
SCONCE*
DESIGNER
ANDREE PUTMAN
MANUFACTURER
*BALDINGER
ARCHITECTURAL LIGHTING
INC.*

PRODUCT
FIGARO
DESIGNER
WINONA LIGHTING
MANUFACTURER
WINONA LIGHTING
DESCRIPTION
POLISHED BRONZE AND
BRASS WITH POLISHED
STAINLESS STEEL ACCENTS
WALL SCONCE
CLIENT
WINONA LIGHTING

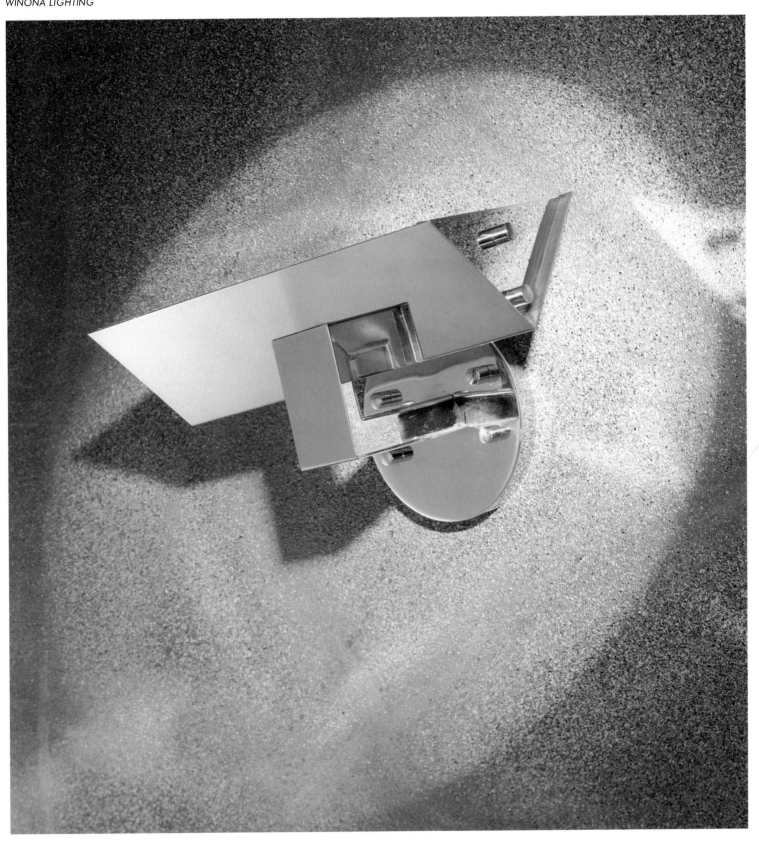

PRODUCT
*COLLAGE FIXTURE/
CHANDELIER*
DESIGNER
*SIRMOS, A DIVISION OF
BROMANTE CORPORATION*
FIRM
*SIRMOS, A DIVISION OF
BROMANTE CORPORATION*
MANUFACTURER
SIRMOS
DESCRIPTION
*RANDOM PATTERN IN
RELIEF ON TULIP-SHAPED
FIXTURE*
PHOTO
SIRMOS

PRODUCT
METAL MEN WALL SCONCE
DESIGNER
BRIAN W. LANDAU
MANUFACTURER
EXPO DESIGN
DESCRIPTION
*ALUMINUM WITH LOW-
VOLTAGE LAMP*
CLIENT
EXPO DESIGN

PRODUCT
LASHTAL SCONCE
DESIGNER
*POURAN ESRAFILY
JOHN BECKMANN*
MANUFACTURER
AXIS MUNDI
DESCRIPTION
*INCANDESCENT LIGHT
SOURCE IS VEILED BY
CHAIN-NAIL FABRIC.*
PHOTO
ARNE SVENSON

PRODUCT
GALILEO
DESIGNER
JAMES EVANSON
DESCRIPTION
*STEEL, COPPER &
HALOGEN*
CLIENT
*AVAILABLE THROUGH ART
ET INDUSTRIE*
PHOTO
JOE COSCIA, JR.

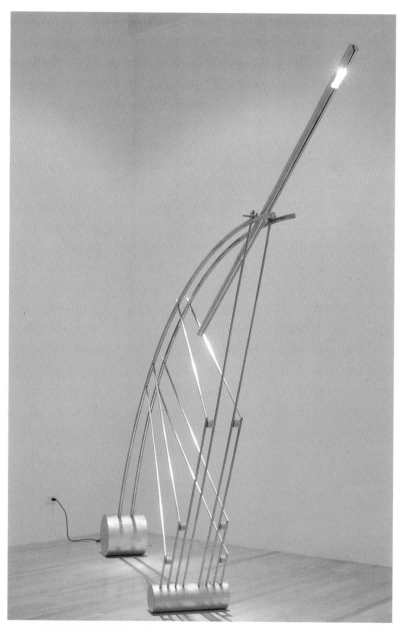

PRODUCT
*"LEAN LAMP" & "LEAN
TWO"*
DESIGNER
ALLEN MIESNER
FIRM
MIESNER DESIGN

PRODUCT
ETERNAL LAMP TWO
ETERNAL LAMP ONE
DESIGNER
GLORIA KISCH
DESCRIPTION
ETERNAL LAMP TWO—
ALUMINUM, BRASS,
STAINLESS & STEEL
ETERNAL LAMP ONE—
STAINLESS, BRASS & STEEL
CLIENT
AVAILABLE THROUGH ART
ET INDUSTRIE
PHOTO
JOE COSCIA, JR.

PRODUCT
UBIQUITY FROM
"APPARITION" SERIES
DESIGNER
TERENCE MAIN
DESCRIPTION
GLASS AND BRONZE LAMP
CLIENT
AVAILABLE THROUGH ART
ET INDUSTRIE
PHOTO
JOE COSCIA, JR.

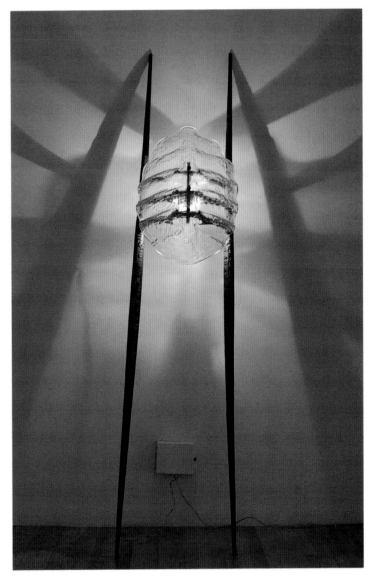

PRODUCT
PEAPOD LAMP
DESIGNER
*HAAS, D'AMATO,
DORFMAN*
DESCRIPTION
*PAINTED STEEL BASE WITH
BRUSHED BRASS FIXTURE
AND PLASTIC*
CLIENT
*AVAILABLE THROUGH
FULLSCALE*

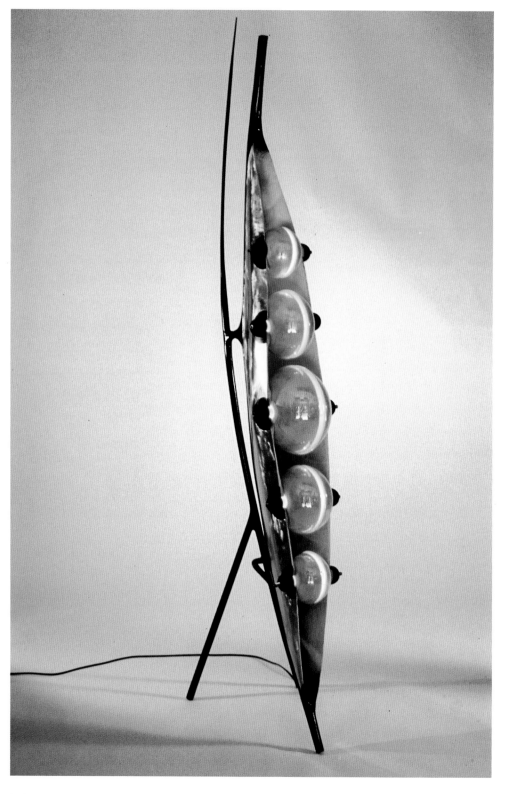

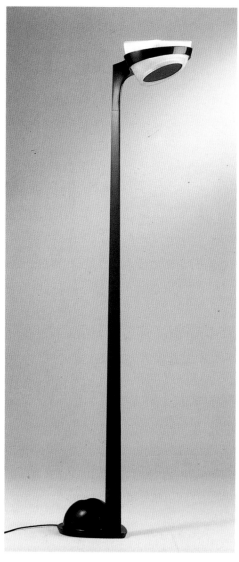

PRODUCT
*GRALL ALPHA FLOOR
LAMP*
DESIGN
*PAOLO FERRARI, LUCIANO
PAGANI AND ANGELO
PERVERSI ASSOCIATES*
MANUFACTURER
FLOS INC.
CLIENT
FLOS INC.

PRODUCT
ARCH
DESIGNER
DAVID BAIRD
FIRM
ZIGGURAT
MANUFACTURER
ZIGGURAT
DESCRIPTION
*TABLE LAMP WITH ETCHED
ALUMINUM STRUCTURE
AND ETCHED GLASS SHELF*
CLIENT
ZIGGURAT
PHOTO
ALAN LINN

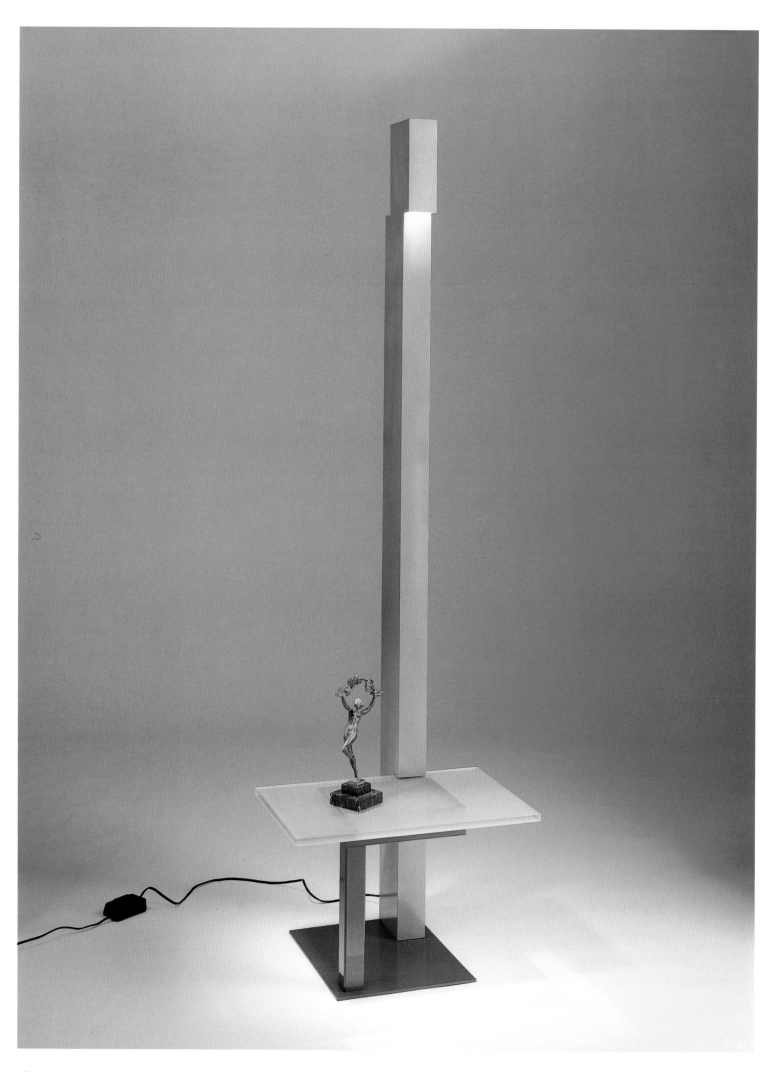

PRODUCT
BIRD HOUSE LIGHT
DESIGNER
JOEL SOKOLOV
DESCRIPTION
*PAINTED WOOD,
PLEXIGLAS, LOG*
PHOTO
JOEL SOKOLOV

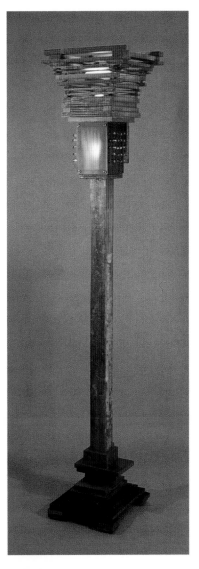

PRODUCT
MARQUEE
DESIGNER
DAVID BAIRD
FIRM
ZIGGURAT
MANUFACTURER
*ZIGGURAT (USA) YAMADA
SHOMEI LIGHTING
(MANUFACTURING FOR
WORLDWIDE EXCEPT USA
DISTRIBUTION)*
DESCRIPTION
*FLOOR LAMP WITH
ETCHED STEEL AND
ALUMINUM STRUCTURE
AND ETCHED GLASS SHELF*
CLIENT
*ROCHE-BOBOIS
INTERNATIONAL, FRANCE*
PHOTO
ALAN LINN

PRODUCT
FOOT-LIGHT
DESIGNER
JOEL SOKOLOV
DESCRIPTION
*PAINTED WOOD,
PLEXIGLAS, AND X-RAY*
PHOTO
JOEL SOKOLOV

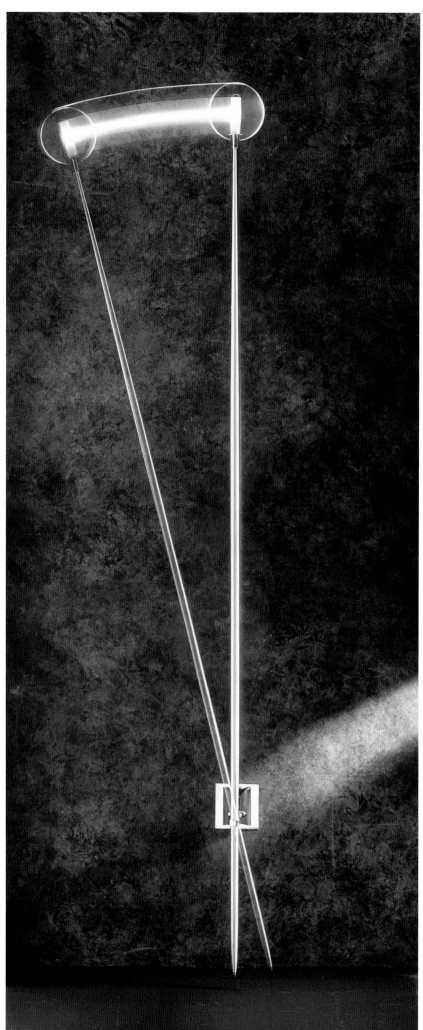

PRODUCT
TESLA WALL LAMP
DESIGNERS
POURAN ESRAFILY
JOHN BECKMANN
MANUFACTURER
AXIS MUNDI
DESCRIPTION
ADJUSTABLE HALOGEN
WALL LAMP
PHOTO
SIMON FELDMAN

PRODUCT
TOLOMEO READING
FLOOR LAMP
DESIGNER
MICHELE DE LUCCHI, GIAN
CARLO FASSINA
MANUFACTURER
ARTEMIDE INC.
DISTRIBUTOR
ARTEMIDE, INC.

PRODUCT
"ANDREA" TORCHIERE
DESIGNER
ANDRZEJ DULJAS
FIRM
KOCH & LOWY
MANUFACTURER
KOCH & LOWY
PHOTO
PETER WEIDLEIN

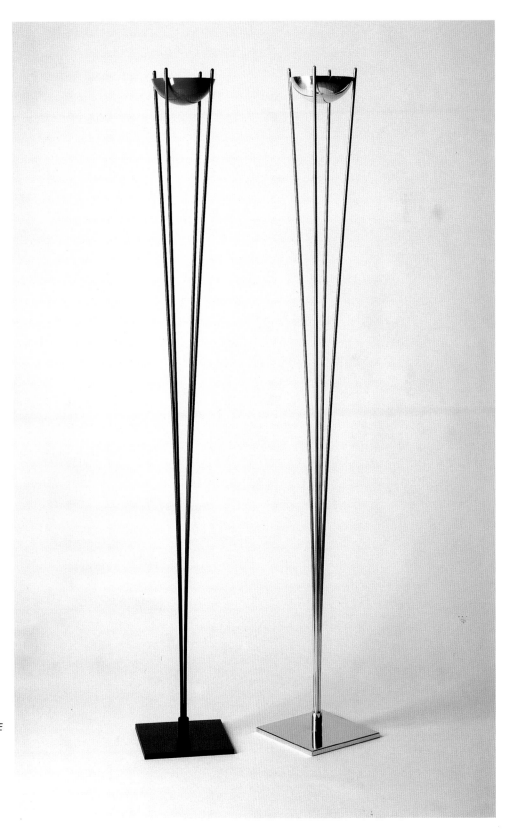

PRODUCT
*FINE ART LAMPS #7906-1,
7871-1, 7901-1*
DESIGNER
MICHAEL WOLK
FIRM
*MICHAEL WOLK DESIGN
ASSOCIATES*
MANUFACTURER
FINE ART LAMPS, INC.
DESCRIPTION
*IRON IN OXIDIZED COPPER
PATINA WITH MATCHING
METAL SHADES*

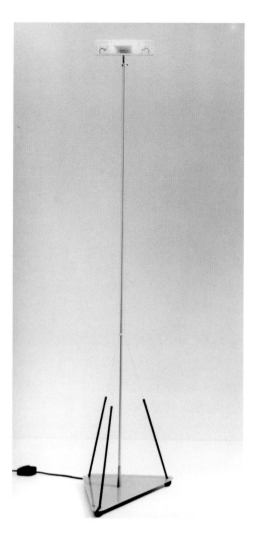

PRODUCT
ACHEO FLOOR
DESIGNER
GIANFRANCO FRATTINI
MANUFACTURER
ARTIMEDE INC.
DESCRIPTION
(see pix 815)
DISTRIBUTOR
ARTEMIDE INC.

PRODUCT
LARRY
DESIGNER
MICHAEL DiBLASI
MANUFACTURER
*GEORGE KOVACS
LIGHTING, INC.*
DESCRIPTION
*SATIN ALUMINUM
PERFORATED SHADE WITH
CLEAR, BLUE, OR GREEN
ACRYLIC RING*
CLIENT
*GEORGE KOVACS
LIGHTING, INC.*

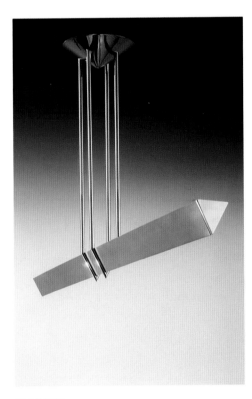

PRODUCT
LINDA PENDANT LAMP
DESIGNER
ANDRÈE PUTMAN
MANUFACTURER
*BALDINGER
ARCHITECTURAL LIGHTING,
INC.*
DESCRIPTION
*A METAL PENDANT LAMP
AVAILABLE IN A BROAD
RANGE OF METAL
FINISHES*
CLIENT
*BALDINGER
ARCHITECTURAL LIGHTING,
INC.*

185

PRODUCT
CYGNET CHANDELIER
DESIGNER
SIRMOS, A DIVISION OF BROMANTE CORPORATION
FIRM
SIRMOS, A DIVISION OF BROMANTE CORPORATION
MANUFACTURER
SIRMOS
DESCRIPTION
TRANSLUCENT RESIN DISC
PHOTO
SIRMOS

PRODUCT
GLORIOSA
DESIGNER
ETTORE SOTTSASS
MANUFACTURER
VENINI
DESCRIPTION
*DECORATOR SUSPENSION
LAMP OF HAND-BLOWN
GLASS AND GOLDEN
METAL ACCESSORIES*
CLIENT
*NORTH AMERICAN
DISTRIBUTOR—HAMPSTEAD
LIGHTING AND
ACCESSORIES, INC.*

PRODUCT
VALANCE OR SCONCE
MANUFACTURER
*CAN-AM MERCHANDISING
SYSTEMS*
DESCRIPTION
*CAN BE USED AS EITHER
LIGHTING FOR A DISPLAY
OR A WALL MOUNTED
DECORATOR LIGHT
FIXTURE*
CLIENT
*CAN-AM MERCHANDISING
SYSTEMS*

PRODUCT
*ALMA, LUCY, TOR & RA
EXPANDED LINE NETWORK
TRACKLIGHTING SYSTEM*
DESIGNER
*PERRY A KING, SANTIAGO
MIRANDA*
MANUFACTURER
FLOS INC.
DESCRIPTION
*FOUR TO SIX INDIVIDUAL
FIXTURES SUSPEND FROM
THE TRACK*
CLIENT
FLOS INC.

PRODUCT
*MIDADO SYSTEM (FULL
VIEW)*
DESIGNER
F.A. PORSCHE
MANUFACTURER
ARTIMEDE LITECH INC.
DESCRIPTION
(see pix 819)
DISTRIBUTOR
ARTEMIDE INC.

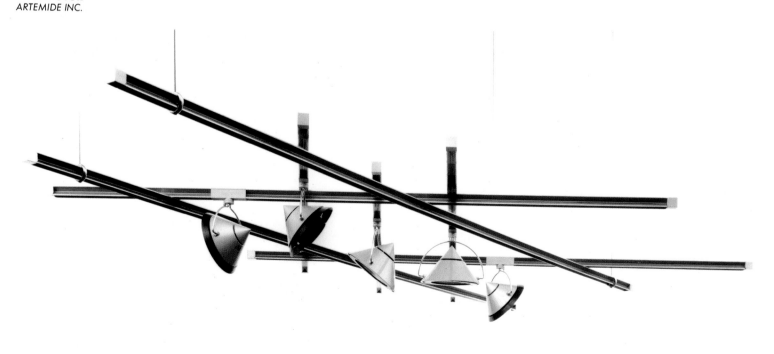

188

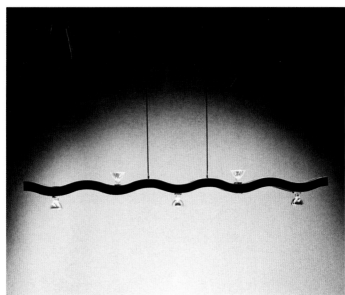

PRODUCT
NESSIE
DESIGN FIRM
DePAS D'URBINO LOMAZZI
MANUFACTURER
STILNOVO
DESCRIPTION
A SUSPENSION LAMP IN LACQUERED BLACK OR GRAY METAL
CLIENT
NORTH AMERICAN DISTRIBUTOR—HAMPSTEAD LIGHTING AND ACCESSORIES, INC.

PRODUCT
TITANIA
DESIGNER
ALBERTO MEDA; PAOLO RIZZATTO
MANUFACTURER
LUCE PLAN
DESCRIPTION
(see pix 813)
DISTRIBUTOR
ARTEMIDE INC.

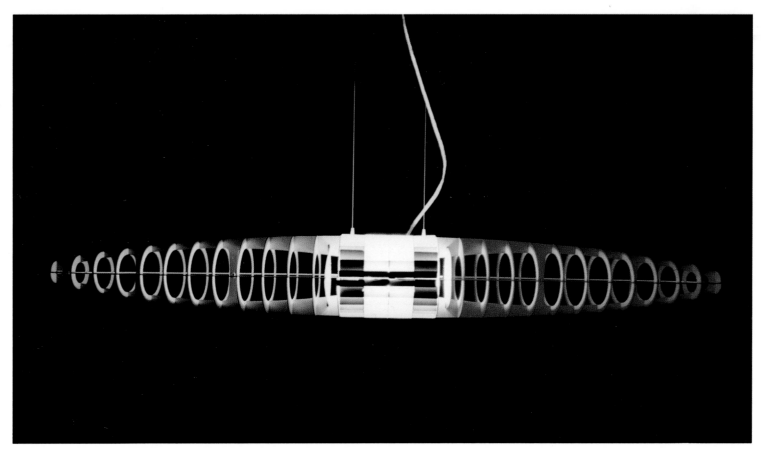

PRODUCT
PRIZZM
MANUFACTURER
DAVIMPORT
DESCRIPTION
*NEON FAN WITH FIVE
CLEAR ACRYLIC BLADES*
CLIENT
DAVIMPORT

PRODUCT
SCALINI
DESIGNER
LIGHTOLIER
MANUFACTURER
LIGHTOLIER
DESCRIPTION
*A PENDALIER OF STACKS
OF CLEAR GLASS*
CLIENT
LIGHTOLIER

PRODUCT
½ LUNA
DESIGNER
RICARDO SALINAS
FIRM
*RICARDO SALINAS
INDUSTRIAL DESIGN*
DESCRIPTION
*ADJUSTABLE QUARTZ
HALOGEN TASK LAMP*
PHOTO
MANUEL HEIBLUM

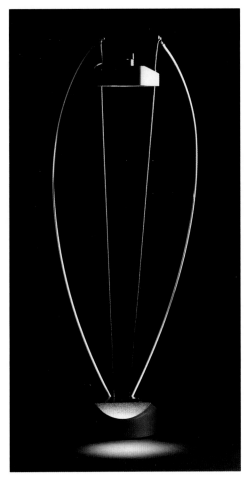

PRODUCT
LYTEJACKS
DESIGNER
LIGHTOLIER
MANUFACTURER
LIGHTOLIER
DESCRIPTION
*LOW-VOLTAGE LIGHTING
SYSTEM*
CLIENT
LIGHTOLIER

191

PRODUCT
PLANET AND TORCH LAMPS
DESIGNER
DON RUDDY

PRODUCT
ALIEN LAMP
DESIGNER
DON RUDDY

PRODUCT
"DEAR FAUSTO" STANDING LAMP (FULL VIEW)
DESIGNER
SHIGERU UCHIDA
FIRM
STUDIO 80
MANUFACTURER
YAMAGIWA CO. LTD.
DESCRIPTION
DEFLECTOR: STEEL W/ BAKED MELAMINE FINISH. BODY: KATSURA WOOD W/ CLEAR LACQUER FINISH
PHOTO
NACÁSA & PARTNERS INC.

PRODUCT
TAIPEI TABLE LAMP
DESIGNER
ROBERTO MARCATTI
FIRM
PREARO LAMPADARI
MANUFACTURER
PREARO LAMPADARI
DESCRIPTION
*TABLE LAMP IN FILIGREED
CRYSTAL PIREX TUBE, WITH
STEEL BASE*
PHOTO
STEFANO MOSNA

PRODUCT
"COBALT"
DESIGNER
PIOTR SIERAKOWSKI
FIRM
KOCH & LOWY
MANUFACTURER
KOCH & LOWY
PHOTO
PETER WEIDLEIN

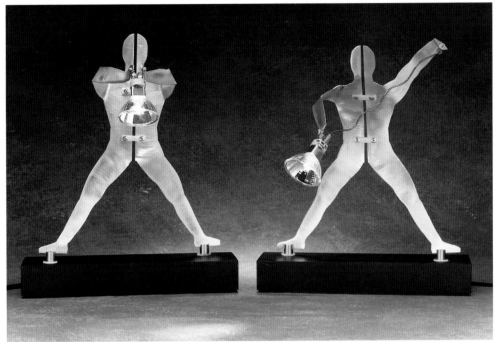

PRODUCT
METAL MEN DESK LAMP
DESIGNER
BRIAN W. LANDAU
MANUFACTURER
EXPO DESIGN
DESCRIPTION
ALUMINUM WITH LOW-VOLTAGE LAMP
CLIENT
EXPO DESIGN

PRODUCT
LINCOLN
DESIGNER
PETER STATHIS
DESCRIPTION
A LAMP THAT IS A MINIMALIST UPDATE OF THE SCONCE
PHOTO
KEN SKALSKI

195

PRODUCT
A120 CHINA
DESIGNER
STEPHAN COPELAND
FIRM
*ATELIER INTERNATIONAL,
LTD.*
MANUFACTURER
*ATELIER INTERNATIONAL,
LTD.*
DESCRIPTION
HALOGEN TASK LAMP
PHOTO
*STUDIO PHOTOGRAPHERS
IN ITALY*

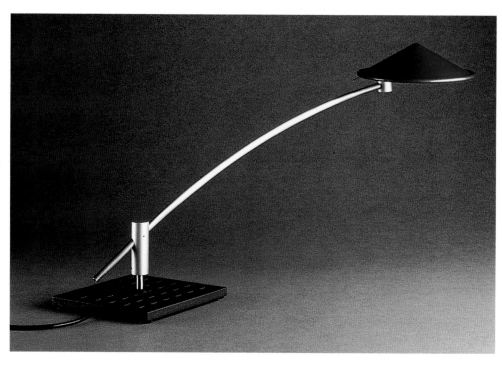

PRODUCT
"VENTOSA"
DESIGNER
MAURIZIO POREGALLI
CLIENT
NOTO
PHOTOGRAPHY
RITETTO-CHIMENTI

PRODUCT
VOL-AU-VENT/S CEILING
LAMP
DESIGNER
AFRA & TOBIA SCARPA
MANUFACTURER
FLOS INC.
DESCRIPTION
GULL-WING EFLECTOR/
DIFFUSER ROTATES 360°
AROUND LAMPHOLDER
CLIENT
FLOS INC.

PRODUCT
A120 CHINA
DESIGNER
STEPHAN COPELAND
FIRM
ATELIER INTERNATIONAL,
LTD.
MANUFACTURER
ATELIER INTERNATIONAL,
LTD.
DESCRIPTION
HALOGEN TASK LAMP
PHOTO
STUDIO PHOTOGRAPHERS
IN ITALY

PRODUCT
*TANGO—TABLE BASE
HALOGEN*
DESIGNER
STEPHAN COPELAND
FIRM
*ATELIER INTERNATIONAL,
LTD.*
MANUFACTURER
*ATELIER INTERNATIONAL,
LTD.*
DESCRIPTION
*TASK LAMP ADJUSTS BY
MEANS OF A UNIQUELY
DETAILED ARTICULATED
JOINT*
PHOTO
*STUDIO PHOTOGRAPHERS
IN ITALY*

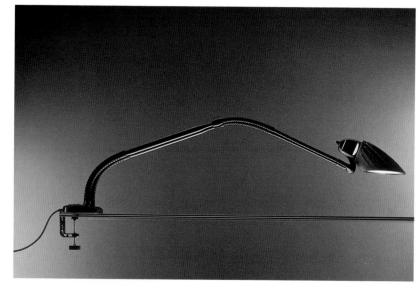

PRODUCT
TANGO
DESIGNER
STEPHAN COPELAND
FIRM
*ATELIER INTERNATIONAL,
LTD.*
MANUFACTURER
*ATELIER INTERNATIONAL,
LTD.*
DESCRIPTION
*TASK LAMP ADJUSTS BY
MEANS OF A UNIQUELY
DETAILED ARTICULATED
JOINT*
PHOTO
*STUDIO PHOTOGRAPHERS
IN ITALY*

DESIGNER
PHILIPPE STARCK
MANUFACTURER
FLOS INC.
CLIENT
FLOS INC.

PRODUCT
PAPER CLIP
DESIGNER
SONNEMAN DESIGN GROUP, INC.
FIRM
SONNEMAN DESIGN GROUP, INC.
MANUFACTURER
GEORGE KOVACS LIGHTING, INC.
DESCRIPTION
HALOGEN DESK LAMP WITH TWO MATTE BLACK RUBBERIZED WIRE RODS EXTENDING FROM A TRIANGULAR BASE. RODS ARE JOINED BY A DELINEATED RED CURVE AND COVERED BY A PERFORATED METAL SHADE
CLIENT
GEORGE KOVACS LIGHTING, INC.
PHOTO
JOSEPH CLEMENTI

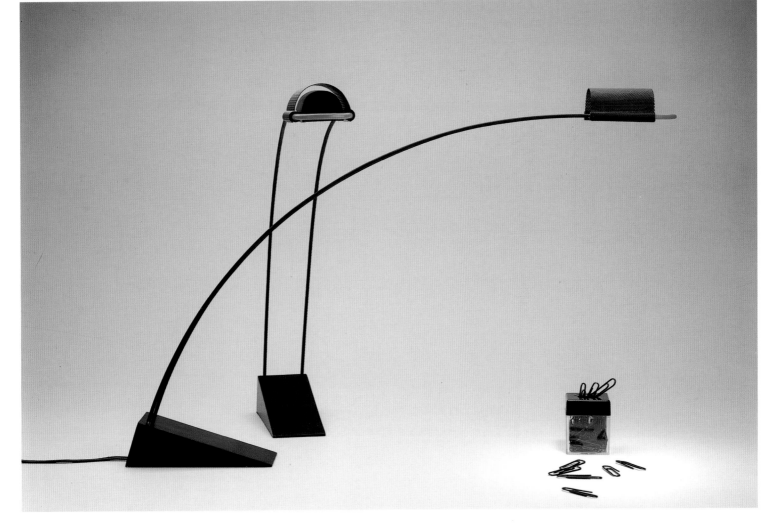

Accessories
Miscellaneous

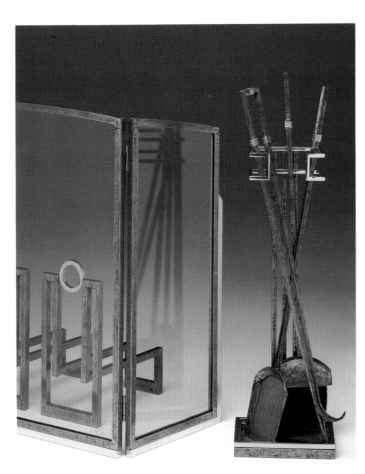

PRODUCT
FIREPLACE ACCESSORIES
DESIGNER
MATTHEW SMYTH
FIRM
LUTEN CLAREY STERN
PHOTO
JOHN BIGELOW TAYLOR

PRODUCT
HIS AND HERS ANDIRONS
DESIGNER
FREDERIC SCHWARTZ
FIRM
*ANDERSON/SCHWARTZ
ARCHITECTS*
MANUFACTURER
SOESBURY FORGE
DESCRIPTION
*HAND-FORGED BLACK
IRON WITH BRASS BALL
ACCENTS*
PHOTO
STEVE MOORE

PRODUCT
CIRCUS WALL CABINET
DESIGNER
IRIS FINGERHUT
DESCRIPTION
*PINE, ACRYLIC PAINT,
REMOVABLE ANIMALS*
PHOTO
NICOLE KATANO

PRODUCT
DRY STORAGE BIN
DESIGNER
IRIS FINGERHUT
DESCRIPTION
PINE, ANILINE DYE
PHOTO
NICOLE KATANO

PRODUCT
BARNYARD WALL CABINET
DESIGNER
IRIS FINGERHUT
DESCRIPTION
PINE, ACRYLIC PAINT,
REMOVABLE ANIMALS
PHOTO
NICOLE KATANO

PRODUCT
NIGHTABLES
DESIGNER
MARK ROBBINS
MANUFACTURER
MARK ROBBINS
DESCRIPTION
*A SERIES OF
ARCHITECTURAL STUDIES
EMPLOYING WEIGHTS,
MIRRORS, AND DOUBLE
HINGED FRAMES. EACH
PIECE TRANSFORMS
REVEALING GEOMETRIC
AND FIGURATIVE
ELEMENTS WITHIN
COVERED INTERNAL
CHAMBERS*
PHOTO
GRANT TAYLOR

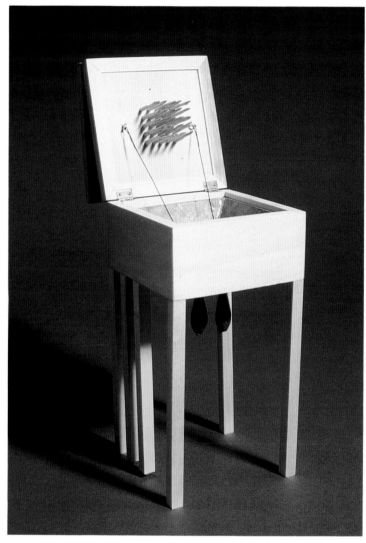

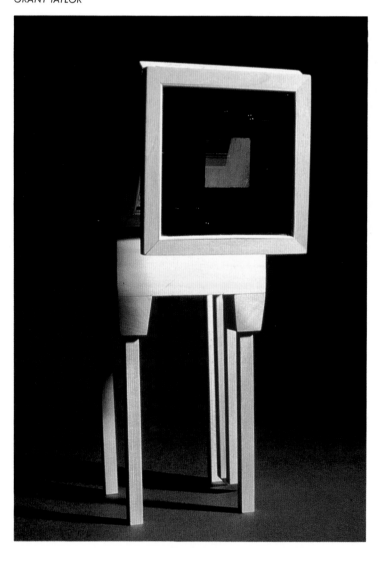

PRODUCT
NIGHTABLES
DESIGNER
MARK ROBBINS
MANUFACTURER
MARK ROBBINS
DESCRIPTION
*A SERIES OF
ARCHITECTURAL STUDIES
EMPLOYING WEIGHTS,
MIRRORS, AND DOUBLE
HINGED FRAMES. EACH
PIECE TRANSFORMS
REVEALING GEOMETRIC
AND FIGURATIVE
ELEMENTS WITHIN
COVERED INTERNAL
CHAMBERS*
PHOTO
GRANT TAYLOR

PRODUCT
NIGHTABLES
DESIGNER
MARK ROBBINS
MANUFACTURER
MARK ROBBINS
DESCRIPTION
A SERIES OF
ARCHITECTURAL STUDIES
EMPLOYING WEIGHTS,
MIRRORS, AND DOUBLE
HINGED FRAMES. EACH
PIECE TRANSFORMS
REVEALING GEOMETRIC
AND FIGURATIVE
ELEMENTS WITHIN
COVERED INTERNAL
CHAMBERS
PHOTO
GRANT TAYLOR

PRODUCT
NIGHTABLES
DESIGNER
MARK ROBBINS
MANUFACTURER
MARK ROBBINS
DESCRIPTION
A SERIES OF
ARCHITECTURAL STUDIES
EMPLOYING WEIGHTS,
MIRRORS, AND DOUBLE
HINGED FRAMES. EACH
PIECE TRANSFORMS
REVEALING GEOMETRIC
AND FIGURATIVE
ELEMENTS WITHIN
COVERED INTERNAL
CHAMBERS
PHOTO
GRANT TAYLOR

PRODUCT
IENA TELEVISION CART
DESIGNER
MATTHEW SMYTH
FIRM
LUTEN CLAREY STERN
DESCRIPTION
SOLID CHERRY ON CASTERS
PHOTO
JOHN BIGELOW TAYLOR

PRODUCT
IENA TELEPHONE TABLE
DESIGNER
MATTHEW SMYTH
FIRM
LUTEN CLAREY STERN
DESCRIPTION
SOLID CHERRY ON
CASTERS
PHOTO
JOHN BIGELOW TAYLOR

PRODUCT
*CONVENTIONAL RECORD
STAND*
DESIGNER
PAUL BRADLEY
DESCRIPTION
MAPLE AND COPPER
CLIENT
OBJECT DESIGN
PHOTO
RICK ENGLISH

PRODUCT
TRESSLE TABLE
DESIGNER
PETER M. DIEPENBROCK
DESCRIPTION
STEEL & GRANITE
PHOTO
JAMES BEARDS

PRODUCT
211 PEDESTAL
DESIGNER
GUIDO RODRIGUEZ
DESCRIPTION
*PLUM PATINATED STEEL
AND JITTERBUGGED
ALUMINUM TOP. SIGNED
AND NUMBERED—LIMITED
EDITION OF 100*
CLIENT
*AVAILABLE THROUGH
FULLSCALE*

209

PRODUCT
*"COBALT SERIES—
DELINEATIONS IN STEEL"*
DESIGNER
PETER DIEPENBROCK
MANUFACTURER
PETER DIEPENBROCK
PHOTO
JAMES BEARDS

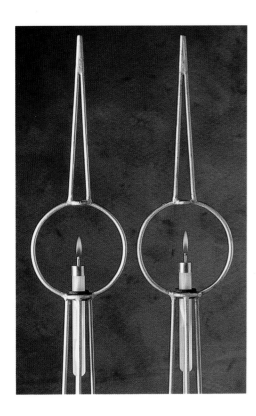

PRODUCT
"COBALT SERIES—
DELINEATIONS IN STEEL"
(DETAIL OF OIL LAMPS)
DESIGNER
PETER DIEPENBROCK
MANUFACTURER
PETER DIEPENBROCK
PHOTO
JAMES BEARDS

PRODUCT
"COBALT SERIES—
DELINEATIONS IN STEEL"
(OIL LAMPS)
DESIGNER
PETER DIEPENBROCK
MANUFACTURER
PETER DIEPENBROCK
PHOTO
JAMES BEARDS

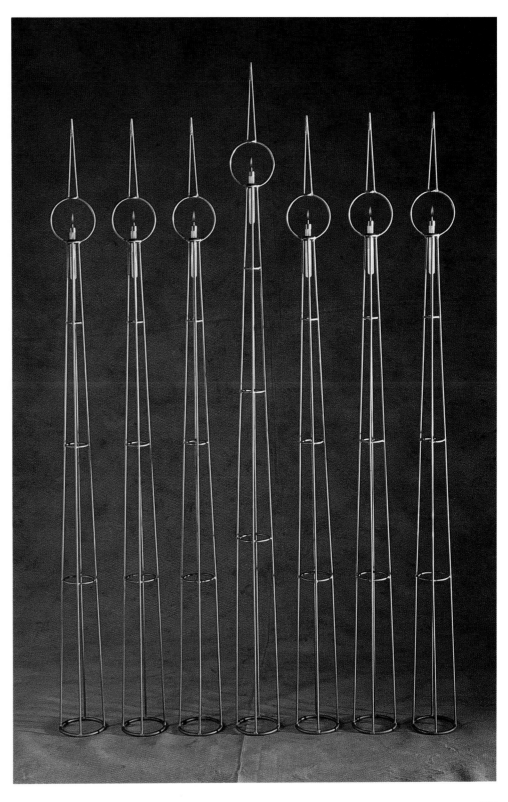

PRODUCT
*THE CLASSICAL URN
REVISITED*
DESIGNER
PETER DIEPENBROCK
MANUFACTURER
PETER DIEPENBROCK
DESCRIPTION
*TWO MATCHING URNS
COMPLETELY FABRICATED
IN STEEL WITH BRASS
GRAZING. EACH URN HAS
A SUB-FLOOR, AND A
REAR-PANEL SECTION
WHICH LIFTS OFF
COMPLETELY TO ALLOW
THE PLACEMENT OF LARGE
POTTED PLANTS OR
TOPIARIES WITHIN THE
URN. THEY HAVE A WIRE-
BRUSH FINISH WITH CLEAR
LACQUER FOR
PROTECTION FROM
OXIDATION.*
CLIENT
*BARBARA MIRMAN-
INTERIOR DESIGNER FOR
DR. PAUL RICHER*
PHOTO
JAMES BEARDS

PRODUCT
AMPHORA
DESIGNER
PETER DIEPENBROCK
MANUFACTURER
PETER DIEPENBROCK
DESCRIPTION
STEEL AMPHORA
PHOTO
JAMES BEARDS

PRODUCT
RING OF FIRE
DESIGNER
RICHARD SNYDER
FIRM
RICHARD SNYDER DESIGN
DESCRIPTION
*AN OVERSIZED
CANDELABRA OF
WROUGHT IRON*
CLIENT
*AVAILABLE THROUGH ART
ET INDUSTRIE*
PHOTOGRAPHY
BILL WHITE

PRODUCT
*CAMELOT STANDING
MIRROR*
DESIGNER
BABETTE HOLLAND
MANUFACTURER
BABETTE HOLLAND
DESCRIPTION
*COPPER AND CAST IRON
MIRROR WITH ALUMINUM
TRIM*
CLIENT
*REPRESENTED BY
FURNITURE OF THE 20TH
CENTURY*

PRODUCT
JIGSAW COAT RACKS
DESIGNER
*JOHN BECKMANN &
POURAN ESRAFILY*
MANUFACTURER
AXIS MUNDI
DESCRIPTION
*FLEXIBLE CARBON-FIBER
RODS WITH NICKEL-PLATED
BRASS INTERLOCKING
JIGSAW PUZZLE-SHAPED
BASES.*
PHOTO
SIMON FELDMAN

PRODUCT
TJIGI-TJIGI
DESIGNER
RICHARD SNYDER
FIRM
RICHARD SNYDER DESIGN
DESCRIPTION
*ETAGERE OF WROUGHT
IRON WITH HAND PAINTED
STEEL DISH INSERTS*
CLIENT
*AVAILABLE THROUGH ART
ET INDUSTRIE*
PHOTO
JOE COSCIA

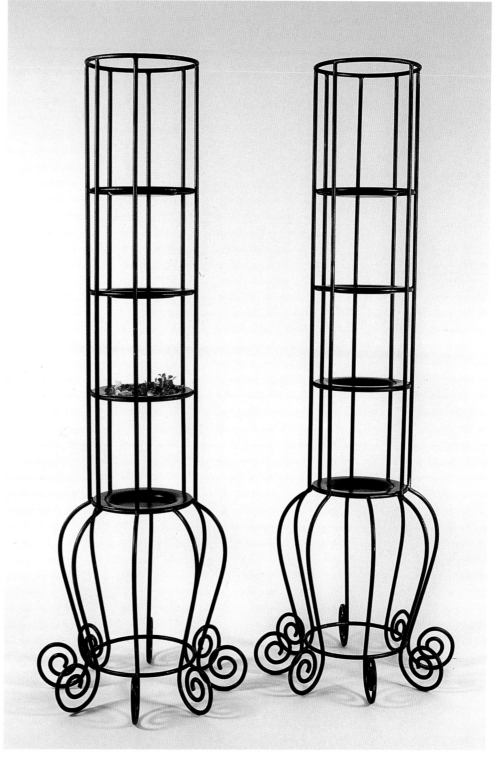

PRODUCT
EXPOSED
DESIGNER
ELEONORA TRIGUBOFF
DESCRIPTION
BRONZE & GLASS
CLIENT
*AVAILABLE THROUGH ART
ET INDUSTRIE*
PHOTO
BEVERLY PARKER

PRODUCT
WATERFALL/LIGHT TOWER
DESIGNER
JOEL SOKOLOV
PHOTO
JOEL SOKOLOV

PRODUCT
VERTEBOWL
DESIGNER
TERENCE MAIN
DESCRIPTION
GLASS AND BRONZE
CLIENT
*AVAILABLE THROUGH ART
ET INDUSTRIE*
PHOTO
JOSEPH COSCIA, JR.

PRODUCT
VASE
DESIGNER
RHEA ALEXANDER
DESCRIPTION
BRASS AND STEEL FRAME, CERAMIC AND GLASS VESSEL
CLIENT
AVAILABLE THROUGH FULLSCALE

PRODUCT
"PEBBLES" AND "BAM-BAM"
DESIGNER
NORMAN CAMPBELL
DESCRIPTION
STEEL AND STONE
CLIENT
AVAILABLE THROUGH ART ET INDUSTRIE
PHOTO
JOSEPH COSCIA, JR.

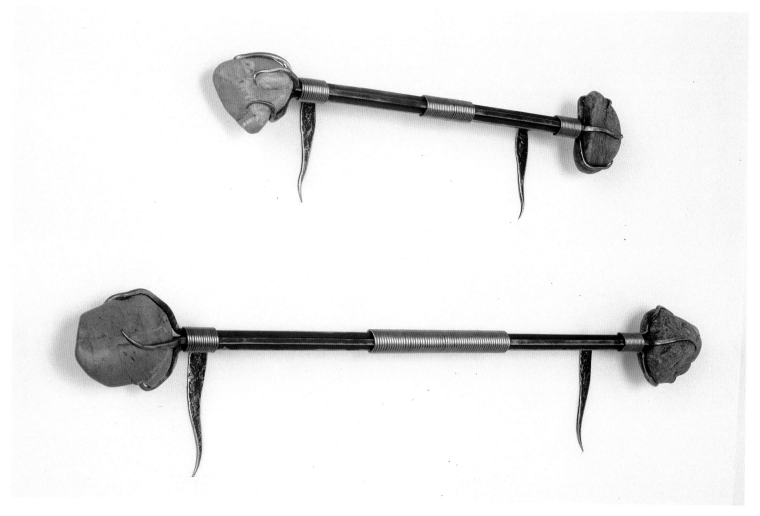

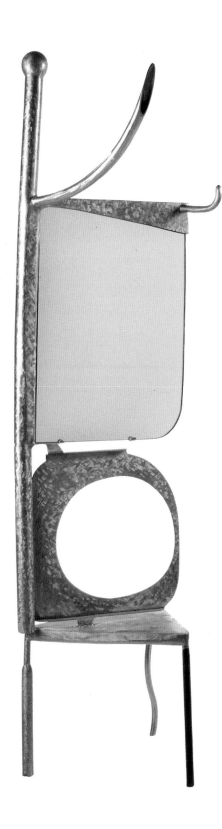

PRODUCT
"IN THE MIRROR"
DESIGNER
GLORIA KISCH
DESCRIPTION
*STEEL, STAINLESS &
MIRROR*
CLIENT
*AVAILABLE THROUGH ART
ET INDUSTRIE*
PHOTO
JOSEPH COSCIA, JR.

PRODUCT
THE TALKING MIRROR
DESIGNER
RICHARD SNYDER
FIRM
RICHARD SNYDER DESIGN
DESCRIPTION
*BEVELLED MIRROR, IN
ROUGHLY TEXTURED
GOLDEN FRAME WITH
SENSOR ACTIVATED
RECORDED SOUND, TELLS
YOU "HOW BEAUTIFUL
YOU ARE" WHEN YOU
"LOOK DEEP INTO THE
MIRROR."*
PHOTO
BILL WHITE

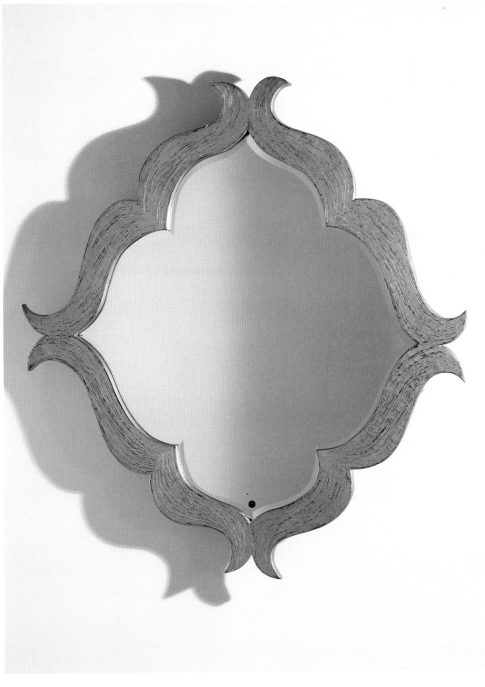

PRODUCT
*LESER MIRROR
COLLECTION*
DESIGNER
MAX LESER
FIRM
BECKER DESIGNED, INC.
MANUFACTURER
BECKER DESIGNED, INC.
DESCRIPTION
*FLOOR AND WALL
MIRRORS WITH 6MM
MIRROR GLASS AND
MACHINED CYLINDRICAL
BASES*
PHOTO
LEN RIZZI

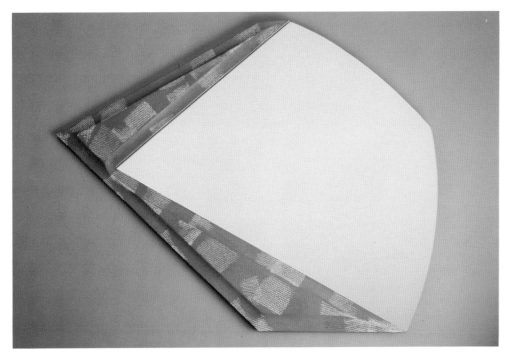

PRODUCT
ABSTRACT MIRROR
DESIGNER
ALAN S. KUSHNER
DESCRIPTION
*STAINED MAHOGANY W/
DECORATIONS*
PHOTO
ALICE SEBRELL

PRODUCT
ABSTRACT WALL MIRROR
DESIGNER
ALAN S. KUSHNER
DESCRIPTION
*STAINED-MAHOGANY,
ZEBRA WOOD, EBONY*
PHOTO
KAREN MAUCH

221

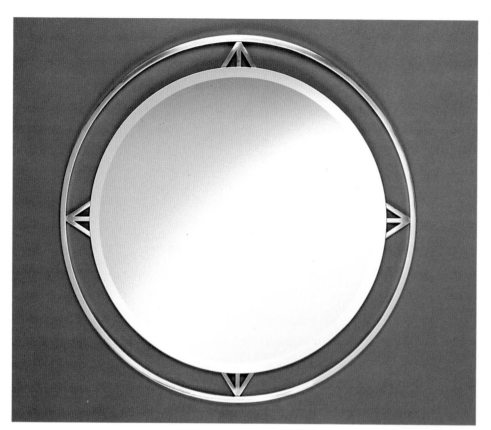

PRODUCT
ETOILE WALL MIRROR
DESIGNER
DAVID ZELMAN
FIRM
PROLOGUE 2000
PHOTO
SIMON FELDMAN

PRODUCT
SILHOUETTE MIRROR
DESIGNER
AL GLASS
FIRM
BECKER DESIGNED, INC.
MANUFACTURER
BECKER DESIGNED, INC.
DESCRIPTION
*WALL MIRROR WITH SHELF
FEATURING 6MM GLASS
AND FORMED
ALUMINUM; IN SILVER OR
BLACK ENAMEL*
PHOTO
LEN RIZZI

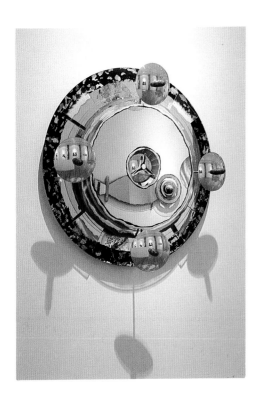

PRODUCT
"NOW YOU DON'T"
DESIGNER
CARMEN SPERA
DESCRIPTION
*MIRROR WITH PIGMENT,
COPPER, WOOD AND
ACRYLIC*
CLIENT
*AVAILABLE THROUGH ART
ET INDUSTRIE*
PHOTO
JOSEPH COSCIA, JR.

PRODUCT
*"INVASION OF A VAIN
CULTURE BY COMMON
STARLING SPIVS"*
FIRM
*THE IMPERIAL
WOODWORKS*

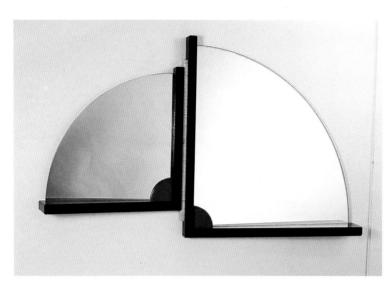

PRODUCT
*RECHERCHÉ SERIES WALL
MIRROR (STYLE E)*
DESIGNER
TOM KNEELAND
FIRM
KNEELAND/SULLIVAN INC.
MANUFACTURER
KNEELAND/SULLIVAN INC.
DESCRIPTION
BUBINGA, BLACK LACQUER
PHOTO
TOM KNEELAND

PRODUCT
*RECHERCHÉ SERIES WALL
MIRRORS (STYLE A)*
DESIGNER
TOM KNEELAND
FIRM
KNEELAND/SULLIVAN INC.
MANUFACTURER
KNEELAND/SULLIVAN INC.
DESCRIPTION
*BUBINGA, SOFT MAPLE,
BLACK LACQUER*
PHOTO
TOM KNEELAND

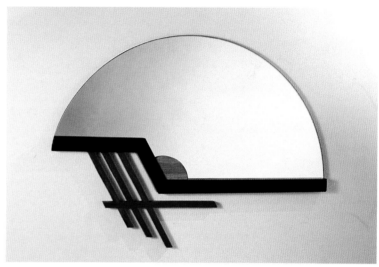

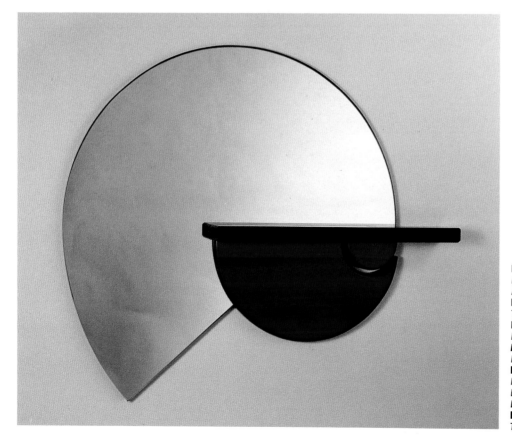

PRODUCT
*RECHERCHÉ SERIES WALL
MIRROR (STYLE C)*
DESIGNER
TOM KNEELAND
FIRM
KNEELAND/SULLIVAN INC.
MANUFACTURER
KNEELAND/SULLIVAN INC.
DESCRIPTION
*PURPLEHEART,
BLOODWOOD, BLACK
LACQUER*
PHOTO
TOM KNEELAND

PRODUCT
WALL CLOCK
DESIGNER
TAKASHI KATOH
DESIGN FIRM
SESSA CO. LTD.
MANUFACTURER
TAKATA, INC.
DESCRIPTION
ALUMINUM WALL CLOCKS

PRODUCT
"DEAR MORRIS" CLOCK
DESIGNER
SHIGERU UCHIDA
FIRM
STUDIO 80
MANUFACTURER
CHAIRS
DESCRIPTION
*MADE OF BIRCH
PLYWOOD WITH A
CORRUGATED FACE AND
PEBBLE FINISH*
PHOTO
NACASA & PARTNERS INC.

PRODUCT
*KRUPS QUARTZ WALL
CLOCK*
DESIGNER
*HIROAKI KOZU, MICHAEL
YOUNG*
FIRM
*MICHAEL W. YOUNG
ASSOC., INC.*
MANUFACTURER
ROBERT KRUPS
CLIENT
ROBERT KRUPS

PRODUCT
*KRUPS QUARTZ WALL
CLOCK*
DESIGNER
*HIROAKI KOZU, MICHAEL
YOUNG*
FIRM
*MICHAEL W. YOUNG
ASSOC., INC.*
MANUFACTURER
ROBERT KRUPS
CLIENT
ROBERT KRUPS

PRODUCT
WALL CLOCK
DESIGNER
MARIANNE FORREST
MANUFACTURER
MARIANNE FORREST
DESCRIPTION
*SANDBLASTED GLASS
WALL CLOCK WITH
CHROME STUDS*
CLIENT
*DOW CHEMICALS,
LONDON*
PHOTO
MARIANNE FORREST

PRODUCT
TABLE CLOCK
DESIGNER
MARIANNE FORREST
MANUFACTURER
MARIANNE FORREST
DESCRIPTION
*SLATE AND SILVER WITH A
LEATHER FACE*
PHOTO
MARIANNE FORREST

228

PRODUCT
*BRASS AND PATINATED
SILVER LEAF WALL CLOCK*
DESIGNER
MARIANNE FORREST
MANUFACTURER
MARIANNE FORREST
DESCRIPTION
*"WORSHIPER 1," INSPIRED
BY RELIGIONS ALL OVER
THE WORLD*
PHOTO
MARIANNE FORREST

PRODUCT
*CONCRETE AND SILVER
LEAF WALL CLOCK*
DESIGNER
MARIANNE FORREST
MANUFACTURER
MARIANNE FORREST
PHOTO
MARIANNE FORREST

PRODUCT
PANS BIRDS SCREEN
DESIGNER
JOEL SOKOLOV
DESCRIPTION

PRODUCT
ROOM DIVIDER
DESIGNER
TOM KNEELAND
FIRM
KNEELAND/SULLIVAN INC.
MANUFACTURER
KNEELAND/SULLIVAN INC.
DESCRIPTION
*LOWER AREA OF ROOM
DIVIDER IS OF PURPLE-
HEART, LACEWOOD,
WENGE AND BLOOD-
WOOD; UPPER AREA IS
KOKOMO GLASS*
PHOTO
NEIL SJOBLOM

PRODUCT
TRANSLUSCENT SCREEN
DESIGNER
NINA SOBELL
DESCRIPTION
*TEXTURED PLEXIGLAS
PANELS IN OAK
FRAMEWORK WITH
LACQUER FINISH.*

PRODUCT
TRANSLUSCENT SCREEN
DESIGNER
NINA SOBELL
DESCRIPTION
*PAINTED (DYES) SYNTHETIC
RICE PAPER IN A BIRCH
FRAMEWORK WITH A
LACQUER FINISH.*

PRODUCT
BIRDS SCREEN (BACK)
DESIGNER
JOEL SOKOLOV
PHOTO
JOEL SOKOLOV

PRODUCT
BIRDS SCREEN (FRONT)
DESIGNER
JOEL SOKOLOV
PHOTO
JOEL SOKOLOV

PRODUCT
REGENT BED
DESIGNER
LOUIS BROMANTE
FIRM
*SIRMOS, A DIVISION OF
BROMANTE CORP.*
MANUFACTURER
SIRMOS
DESCRIPTION
*INSPIRED BY FRENCH
REGENCY PERIOD*
PHOTO
SIRMOS
AWARD
ROSCOE AWARD

PRODUCT
ROYAL OAK BED AND GATE
DESIGNER
BABETTE HOLLAND
MANUFACTURER
BABETTE HOLLAND
DESCRIPTION
COPPER AND CAST IRON FINIALS
CLIENT
REPRESENTED BY FURNITURE FOR THE 20TH CENTURY
PHOTO
ALEX MCLEAN

PRODUCT
REVERIE BED
DESIGNER
BABETTE HOLLAND
MANUFACTURER
BABETTE HOLLAND
DESCRIPTION
COPPER AND CAST IRON BED
CLIENT
REPRESENTED BY FURNITURE FOR THE 20TH CENTURY
PHOTO
DAVID PHELPS
AWARD
USED IN A ROOM DESIGN BY SANTO LAQUASTO FOR THE METROPOLITAN HOME DIFFA HOUSE

PRODUCT
*STEEL, BRASS, SILICON
BRONZE BED*
DESIGNER
PHILIP MILLER
CLIENT
*STEVE ESHERMAN AND
CAMI TAYLOR*
PHOTO
PHILIP MILLER

PRODUCT
BED
DESIGNER
DALE BROHOLM
MANUFACTURER
DALE BROHOLM
PHOTO
POWELL PHOTOGRAPHY

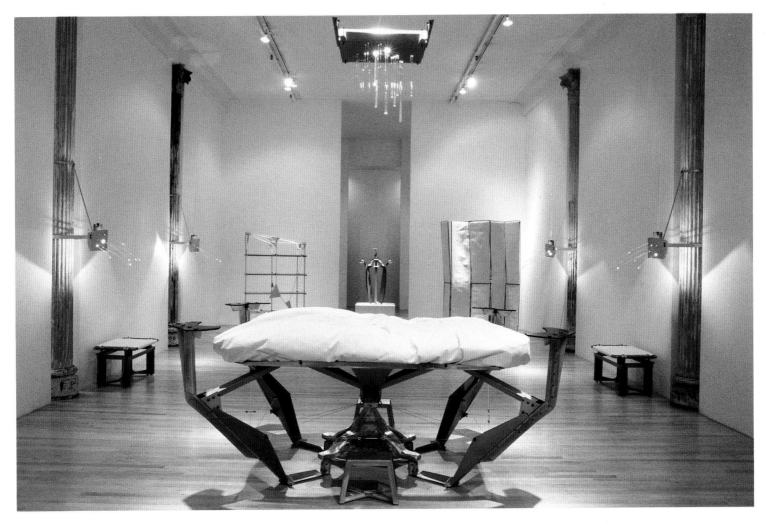

INDEX

DESIGNER

FIRM

PHOTOGRAPHER

DISTRIBUTOR